Thomas M. Anderson

The Political Conspiracies Preceding the Rebellion

Or, the True Stories of Sumter and Pickens

Thomas M. Anderson

The Political Conspiracies Preceding the Rebellion
Or, the True Stories of Sumter and Pickens

ISBN/EAN: 9783337133764

Printed in Europe, USA, Canada, Australia, Japan

Cover: Foto ©Suzi / pixelio.de

More available books at **www.hansebooks.com**

THE

POLITICAL CONSPIRACIES
PRECEDING THE REBELLION

OR

THE TRUE STORIES OF SUMTER
AND PICKENS

BY

THOMAS M. ANDERSON
LIEUT. COL. U. S. A.

———

NEW YORK
G. P. PUTNAM'S SONS
27 & 29 WEST 23D STREET
1882

DEDICATION

TO THE OLD FRIENDS OF

GENERAL ROBERT ANDERSON

THIS MONOGRAPH IS RESPECTFULLY INSCRIBED BY

THE AUTIIOR

CHAPTER I.

"O Conspiracy !
Sham'st thou to show thy dangerous brow by night,
When evils are most free ?   Oh ! then, by day
Where wilt thou find a cavern dark enough
To mask thy monstrous visage ?   Seek none, Conspiracy ;
Hide it in smiles and affability :
For if thou put thy native semblance on,
Not Erebus itself were dim enough
To hide thee from prevention."
JULIUS CÆSAR.

I PURPOSE in this monograph to give an account of the political conspiracies immediately preceding the Rebellion of 1861 against the authority of the National Government of the United States of America.

It would be absurd to assume that one of the greatest civil wars of modern times was the result of conspiracies.

The causes which led to it were far too deep and strong to be controlled by the machinations of politicians.

Nevertheless the outbreak of the Rebellion was preceded by a number of conspiracies the object of which, so far as the Southern leaders were concerned, was to gain certain advantages by cunning and *finesse* before they resorted to the arbitrament of war.

These plots are naturally connected with the sieges of Forts Sumter and Pickens, with which the struggle began.

In regard to the mere physical facts of the siege of Sumter there is no mystery or dispute. But as to the political history which gives it importance, as to the complications which culminated in the first passage at arms in the war, there has been almost as much discussion as there has been as to the guilt or innocence of Mary of Scotland.

What pledges, if any, did Mr. Buchanan give to the South Carolina Commissioners?

What understanding, if any, did he have with Messrs. Barnwell, Adams, and Orr as to the reenforcement or evacuation of the forts in Charleston Harbor?

What pledges, if any, did Mr. Seward subsequently give in relation to Sumter?

Was Major Robert Anderson, its commander, deterred by orders or by his sympathy with the South from opening fire on the Confederates when they began placing batteries around him?

All these questions have been mooted and discussed heretofore with much less intelligence than zeal.

Now at last the publication of the official records gives us a fair, critical, and historical standpoint.

After the October elections in the fall of 1860 had been carried by the Republicans, the election of Mr. Lincoln in November became a foregone conclusion. Knowing this, the people of South Carolina took no pains to conceal their intention of seceding from the Federal Union as soon as the result of the Presidential election was known. As the day of the election approached, the people of Charleston manifested such a turbulent and rebellious spirit, that the engineer officer in charge of the construction parties working on the forts in the harbor asked for permission to arm a number of his workmen to protect the ordnance and ammunition stored in Fort Sumter.

On the 1st of October (1860) the Chief of Ordnance wrote to Mr. Floyd, the Secretary of War, recommending that the request of the engineer officer be complied with, provided it met the approval of the commanding officer of Fort Moultrie. Singularly enough Mr. Floyd approved this application.

The commanding officer of Fort Moultrie, when the matter was referred to him, gave a very hesitating approval of the application, ex-

pressing grave doubts of the loyalty and relia-
bility of the workmen engaged on the forts,
and closed his letter (written November 8th)
by a recommendation that the garrison of Moultrie should be re-enforced, and that both Forts
Sumter and Castle Pinckney should be garrisoned at once by companies sent from Old Point
Comfort (Fort Monroe).   Subsequently he ordered the ordnance officer at the Charleston
Arsenal to turn over to him, for removal to Moultrie, all the small arms and fixed ammunition he
had in store.   The attempt to make this transfer was successfully resisted by the Charleston
mob, and the attempt abandoned.

This action of the commander of the troops
in the harbor, and his application for re-enforcements, led to his prompt removal.   The officer
thus summarily dealt with was Lieut. Colonel
J. L. Gardner, 1st Artillery, a native of Massa-
chusetts, and an old veteran who had entered
the service in 1813.   The South Carolina Commissioners, in their correspondence with President Buchanan, reminded him, with scant cour-
tesy, that Colonel Gardner had been removed
at the dictation of the South Carolina delegates,
because he had called for re-enforcements and
recommended the occupation of Fort Sumter
and Castle Pinckney.

Major Robert Anderson was ordered to relieve this officer and take command of Fort Moultrie on November 15, 1860.

If the Southern cabal that controlled the War Department supposed that he would prove more pliant and less loyal than his predecessor they soon discovered their mistake.

Robert Anderson was born in Kentucky in 1805. Both his father's and mother's family came from England to Virginia in 1635, and removed from Virginia to Kentucky at the close of the War of Independence.[1]

Eight of his blood relations were officers in the Continental Army. His father, the Lieut.-Colonel of the 1st Virginia Continental Infantry, had been wounded at the battles of Trenton and Savannah, and, singularly enough, had fought at Charleston and had been taken prisoner there by the British.

He subsequently acted as A. D. C. to General Lafayette in his campaign against Cornwallis that ended in the siege and capture of Yorktown.

At the close of the Revolutionary War he

---

[1] Major Anderson's relatives in the Continental Army were: R. C. Anderson, Lieut.-Col. 1st Va.; Capt. John Anderson, 3d Va. Inft.; Capt. Wm. Croghan, 4th Va. Inft.; Capt. John Marshall, 7th Va. Inft. (afterward Chief-Justice U. S.); Brig.-Genl. George Rodger Clark; Lieut.-Col. Jonathan Clark, 8th Va. Inft.; Capt. Geo. Anderson, provisional navy.

The members of his family who were officers of the Regular and Volunteer forces, during the war of the Rebellion were as follows:

was selected by the officers of the Continental Army to survey and locate the generous gift of public land given to them by the State of Virginia. This selection was, I believe, made at the first meeting of the Society of the Cincinnati. That he might carry out this work, he was made first Surveyor-General of the Virginia military land district.

This present of land was all that the Continental officers received for their seven years' service in the war for independence. In proposing one of their number to apportion to each his distributive share, they naturally selected a man in whose integrity and justice they had perfect confidence.

This high sense of honor Major Anderson inherited from his father. A more honest, honorable, and chivalrous man never lived. He was a Southerner,[1] and in a proper sense

---

Brig.-Genl. Robert Anderson; Col. Chas. Anderson, 63d Ohio Vol. (subsequently Governor of Ohio); Col. N. L. Anderson, 6th Ohio Vol.; Col. A. L. Anderson, 1st Cal. Vol.; Capt. Wm. P. Anderson, 6th Ohio Vol. (A. A. G. Dept. of Ohio); Capt, E. L. Anderson, A. D. C.; Maj.-Genl. Stanley; Capt. F. P. Anderson, A. D. C.; Maj.-Genl. Schofield; Capt. H. R. Anderson, 3d U. S. Vol.; Major John Simpson, 154th Ind. Vol.; Lieut.-Col. Thomas M. Anderson of the Regular Army; Surg. Richard Logan, Ky. Vol., U. S. A.

[1] The following are the more prominent officers of our army and navy who, although Southerners by birth, remained faithful to the National Government.

In the Army: Winfield Scott, Geo. H. Thomas, Ord, Pope, Rosseau, Meigs, Harney, Frank Blair, Buchanan, Buford, Bayard, R. H. Williams, McKeever, Jos. Taylor, Jas. Marten, Easton,

was a Southern sympathizer. He loved his
State and he loved his friends, and, from accidental associations, most of his friends were
Southerners. But few men ever lived who came
so near having no political opinions and sympathies whatever. He probably never voted in his
life. He used to say that his father's religion
and General Washington's politics were good
enough for him. The Ten Commandments,
the Constitution of the United States, and the
Army Regulations were his guides in life. For
the subject of this essay, for the political problem which his conduct subsequently brought to
the test of practical solution, he cared as little
as any man of his day.

He was sincerely religious and a soldier of
antique character and courage. Above all, he
was a follower of his flag. To him it was like
a sacrament, an outward sign of an inward grace.
It was his symbol of duty. He always saw upon
its folds " In hoc signo vinces."

In the war that followed, eleven of his immedi-

Tompkins, Murray, Cuyler, Simons, Wm. Hammond, J. F. Ham-
mond, Newton, Benit, Laidley, Baylor, Davidson, Royall, E. B.
Alexander, A. J. Alexander, Dent, Getty, T. L. Crittenden, Marrow,
Elwell Otis, Lugenbeel, Dodge, Sprig, Carroll, Cooke, Ramsey, Holt,
Brice, T. J. Wood, Emery, Paul, McIntosh, R. W. Johnson Lang,
Seawell, Hunter, French, Graham (old Pike), Burke (old Martin).

In the Navy: Farragut, John Rodgers, Patterson, Fairfax, Hop-
kins, Carter, Burrett, Young, Jouett, Russell, Stribling, Powell,
Craven, Radford, Turner, Lee, Jenkins, Sands, Steedman, Taylor,
Scott, Stembel, Middleton, Bache, Horner, Ward, Palmer, and
Harlan, all of high rank.

ate family, including himself, held commissions in the Union Army.

With these antecedents and influences, it would have been strange indeed if Robert Anderson had not been loyal to his country.

Nevertheless it is true, beyond reasonable doubt, that the Secretary of War, when he sent him to take command of the forces in Charleston Harbor, fully believed that he would obey all his orders and finally throw his fortunes with the South.

The first letter he received from Major Anderson after he assumed command of Moultrie, dated November 23, 1860, must have shaken his faith.

In it he explains the gravity of the situation and the inadequacy of his means of defence; expresses the conviction that the people of South Carolina intended to seize all the forts in the harbor by force of arms as soon as their ordinance of secession was published; he enlarges on the importance of Sumter and Castle Pinckney, demands reinforcements, notifies the War Department that he will send in a requisition for a supply of ordnance for *all* the forts, and says, finally : " Fort Sumter and Castle Pinckney *must* be garrisoned immediately if the government determines to keep command of the harbor." The italics are his (page 76, vol. i, " Rebellion Records").

In passing through Washington City on his way to Charleston, Major Anderson had seen President Buchanan and the Secretary of War. By the latter at least he had been cautioned to avoid all collision with the people of Charleston, to avoid disturbance, not to excite them, and so on, in this strain of conciliatory weakness. His subsequent letters and instructions were all pitched in the same key.

There is no telling what disapproval and reproof Major Anderson's first letter might not have brought down on his head, for a much less decided letter had caused the removal of Colonel Gardner, had not a new and unexpected element been introduced into the controversy.

The venerable patriot, Lewis Cass, the Secretary of State, suddenly denounced submission as treasonable, and supported Major Anderson's demand for reinforcements. Two other members of the Cabinet seem to have supported Mr. Cass. This was a political bomb-shell, and with this begins the political history of the Sumter episode.

To appreciate fully the situation we must recall the names of the men then in power at Washington.

James Buchanan and John C. Breckenridge were President and Vice-President. Buchanan's first Cabinet were Cass, Cobb, Floyd, Toucey, Thompson, Holt, and Black. Jefferson Davis was Chairman of the Military Committee in the Senate. The men in control of the War Department were Floyd, Cooper, Joe Johnson, Taylor, Craig, De Russy, Don Carlos Buell, Fitz-John Porter, and Withers.

In the Cabinet, Cobb, Floyd, Toucey, and Thompson were rebels or submissionists. They had the ear of the President. In the War Department, Floyd, Cooper, Johnson, Taylor, and Withers were Southerners. Taylor, Craig, and De Russy were loyal, but had no influence. Buell and Porter afterward proved loyal, but at that time were in Floyd's confidence, or at least Floyd had confidence in them. Porter, then Assist. Adjutant-General, made an inspection of the forts in Charleston Harbor a few days before Anderson reached there. His attention had evidently been called to the importance of Castle Pinckney by Colonel Gardner, for in his report he says of it :

" Castle Pinckney commands Charleston, and its armament is complete. Here the powder belonging to the arsenal in the city is stored. A company can be accommodated here, while a small force under an officer would secure it against surprise or even a bold attack of such enemies likely to undertake it."

But he had not the moral courage to recommend its occupation. The report closes with this sentence and signature of evil omen : " Under present circumstances I would not recommend its occupation. Very respectfully, etc., F.-J. Porter, Assistant Adjt.-General " (page 72, *Ibid.*).

Why not recommend it ? Oh, bitter shame to us !

Within two months we have a set of so-called Commissioners writing to the President of this nation these insulting words :

" For the last sixty days you have had in Charleston Harbor not force enough to hold the forts against an equal enemy. Two of them were empty, one of those two the most important in the harbor; it could have been taken at any time. You ought to know better than any man that it would have been taken but for the efforts of those who put their trust in your honor." Signed. " Barnwell, Adams, Orr."

Thanks to this peace-at-any-price policy, this was an insult we had to endure. The circumstance that prevented an officer of the United States Army from recommending the occupation of a United States fort, was the threat of a rebel mob.

General Porter's report was written on the 11th of November. On the 12th Mr. Humphries, the ordnance store-keeper at Charleston Arsenal, writes to the Chief of Ordnance:

" Sir.—In view of the excitement now existing in this city and State, and the possibility of an insurrectionary movement on the part of the servile population, the governor has tendered, through General Schnierle, of South Carolina Militia, a guard of a detachment of a lieutenant and twenty men for this post, which has been accepted."

What delightful protection ! How disinterested ! The wolves offer to protect this pet lamb against the geese ! On the 20th, Brevet Colonel Benjamin Huger,[1] U. S. A., soon of the C. S. A., assumes command of the arsenal by order ; he writes back at once "that Mr. Humphries' prudence and discretion meet his commendation." So a wolf in sheep's clothing was sent down to defend the fold.

Next in order we have a letter from S. Cooper, Adjutant-General, *U. S. A.*, soon to be

[1] Huger, pronounced Hugee. Benj. Huger was a graduate of the Military Academy in the class of 1825. He was twice brevetted for gallantry in battle in the Mexican war. He resigned from the Federal army in 1861, was made a Major-General in the Confederate army, and led the advance of Lee's army at the battle of Malvern Hill.

Adjutant-General, *C. S. A.*, asking Anderson as to the condition "*of the work under his command*" (Fort Moultrie).

In reply (November 28th), Major Anderson politely intimates that he considers himself in command of *all* the works in the harbor, and will put in estimates for ordnance to arm them all.

"Your letter," he says, "confines my answer to what refers *to the work under my charge*. I cannot but remark that I think its security from attack would be more greatly increased by throwing garrisons into Castle Pinckney and Fort Sumter than by any thing that can be done in strengthening the defences of this work." Further on he says, in reply to the suggestion of the honorable Secretary of War about th ex-pediency of employing reliable persons not con-nected with the military service for purposes of fatigue and police, "I must say that I doubt whether such could be obtained here." This was a patriotic suggestion of the Hon. J. B. Floyd, who subsequently resigned his place in the Cabinet because President Buchanan had re-fused to adhere to his promise as Secretary of War, that the forts in Charleston Harbor should not be reinforced or their status changed.

Mr. Floyd fully intended in this way to se-cure the forts in the harbor to the Charleston

people.   For the same reason he allowed the
work of construction and repair to be carried on
by the Engineers.   He knew that the people of
South Carolina had declared their intention of
seizing the forts as soon as their State Convention had passed their ordinance of secession.
Yet with charming consistency we find him
sending this telegram to Captain Foster of the
Engineers :

I have just received a telegraphic dispatch informing
me that you have removed forty muskets from Charleston Arsenal to Fort Moultrie.   If you have removed any
arms return them *instantly*.   Answer by telegraph
                            JOHN B. FLOYD,
                                        Secretary of War.

Colonel Huger had pledged himself to the
Governor of South Carolina that no arms should
be removed from the arsenal.

The Secretary's telegram was dated December
19, 1860, the day before the South Carolina
ordinance of secession was passed.

All of the occurrences above narrated were
prior to this portentous date.

Did President Buchanan know of these
pledges and orders?   Did they have his concurrence and approval?   Or did he, as Judge
Black now asserts, wish to send reinforcements
to Major Anderson ?

On December 8th, four of the members of the South Carolina Congressional delegation went to see the President about the forts in Charleston Harbor. On the 9th, five of them signed the following joint note :

His Excellency, JAMES BUCHANAN,
President of the United States :

In compliance with our statement to you yesterday, we now express to you our strong convictions that neither the constituted authorities, nor any body of the people of the State of South Carolina, will either attack or molest the United States forts in the harbor of Charleston previously to the action of the Convention, and, we hope and believe, not until an offer has been made, through an accredited representative, to negotiate for an amicable arrangement of all matters between the State and Federal Government, provided that no reinforcement shall be sent into those forts, and their relative military status shall remain as at present.

JOHN McQUEEN,
WM. PORCHER MILES,
M. L. BONHAM,
W. W. BOYCE,
LAWRENCE M. KEITT.

Washington, December 9, 1860.

In Mr. Buchanan's letter to Barnwell, Adams, and Orr, the South Carolina Commissioners, written December 31, 1860, after quoting the above letter and referring to the interview that followed, he says : " It is well known that it was my determination, and this I freely expressed, not to reinforce the forts in the harbor, and thus produce a collision, until they had been actually attacked, or until I had certain evidence that they were about to to be attacked." (Page 117, *Ibid.*)

Further on, in reply to their demand for the withdrawal of all the troops from the harbor, he said : "This I cannot do ; this I will not do. Such an idea was never thought of by me in any possible contingency."

As to this statement, the South Carolina Commissioners and two of the South Carolina Congressmen, Miles and Keitt, gave the President the lie circumstantial, if not the lie direct. ("Rebellion Records," pp. 120 to 128, vol. i.)

In this connection the Commissioners wrote to him : "You did not reinforce the garrisons in the harbor of Charleston. You removed a distinguished and veteran officer from the command of Fort Moultrie because he attempted to increase his supply of ammunition. You refused to send additional troops to the same garrison when applied for by the officer appointed to succeed him. You accepted the resignation of the oldest and most efficient member of your Cabinet rather than allow these garrisons to be strengthened. You compelled an officer sta-

tioned at Fort Sumter to return immediately to
the arsenal forty muskets which he had taken
to arm his men." General Cass had resigned
his office of Secretary of State on the 17th of
December, 1860, for the avowed reason that
the President had refused to reinforce Anderson, and was negotiating with open and avowed
traitors.

In 1812 General Cass had, in conjunction
with General McArthur, preferred charges
against General Hull for surrendering a United
States fort to a foreign enemy. He could not,
with any consistency, consent, as a Cabinet
Minister, to the adoption of a line of policy
that would legitimately lead to a surrender of
important defensive works to a domestic foe.
But so far Mr. Buchanan's course had been con-
sistent with his declaration in his annual message, " that he had no right, and would not attempt, to coerce a seceding State."

How did it happen that he so soon laid
himself open to charges of tergiversation, in-
consistency, and duplicity ?

We must turn back a little and refer to some
earlier events, now necessary to consider. Major Anderson had been sent to Charleston by
order of Lieutenant-General Scott. Before this
order had been issued, Anderson had been sum-

moned to Washington by telegraph (November 12th). His order to relieve Colonel Gardner was dated : Headquarters of the Army, New York City, November 15, 1860.

Anderson's first official letter was sent through the regular channels. But he was ordered by the Secretary of War, November 28th, to address his communications in future *only* to the Adjutant-General or *direct* to the Secretary (page 77). From this time forth Major Anderson could only communicate with the enemies of his government, and could only receive his orders from those who were plotting its destruction. It is only fair to remember this, in considering Judge Black's assertion that General Scott was responsible for the failure to reinforce Sumter.

There is reason to believe that the President himself was not made acquainted with all that was transpiring.

On December 27th the following message was delivered to the President from General Scott.

Since the formal order, unaccompanied by special instructions, assigning Major Anderson to the command of Fort Moultrie, no order, intimation, suggestion, or communication for his government and guidance has gone to that officer, or any of his subordinates, from the Headquarters of the Army ; nor have any reports or communications been addressed to the General-in-Chief from Fort Moultrie later than a letter written by Major Anderson almost immediately after his arrival in Charleston Harbor, reporting the then state of the work.

G. W. LAY,
Lieutenant-Colonel, A. D. C.

The President of the United States.

If General Scott and the country at large were kept in ignorance of Major Anderson's wish to occupy Sumter, the leading rebels were not. At the interview of the South Carolina delegation with Mr. Buchanan, on December 9th, one of them explained to him what they meant in their letter by the expression, " *Relative military status* " ; they mentioned the difference between Anderson occupying Forts Moultrie and Sumter. They stated that the latter would be equivalent to reinforcing the garrison, and would, just as certainly as the sending of fresh troops, " lead to the result which we both desired to avoid." (*Vide* Miles and Keitt's statement, page 127.) They added : " When we rose to go, the President said, in substance, ' After all, this is a matter of honor among gentlemen. I do not know that any paper or writing is necessary. We understand each other.' "

In the President's letter of December 31st, before referred to he does not deny the understanding, but he justifies his change of policy by the statement, that, in transferring his command from Moultrie to Sumter, Anderson " had acted on his own responsibility and without authority, unless indeed he had tangible evidence of a design to proceed to a hostile act on the part of the authorities of South Carolina, which has not yet been alleged. He adds in substance that he would have ordered Anderson back if the South Carolina people had not taken the law in their own hands and occupied the other forts. This was mere excuse and evasion, and it must have been deeply humiliating to the President to have to resort to it.

Major Anderson occupied Sumter on the night of December 26th, six days after the South Carolina act of secession, and the day before the Commissioners reached Washington.

The Carolina people feared the move, although they thought, that as Major Anderson was a Southerner, the Secretary of War could control him. Nevertheless they had steam-vessels patrolling the harbor to prevent the crossing.

The North was surprised and delighted at this bold move, because it was not generally known that the occupation of Sumter had been contemplated and advised by Major Anderson.

The rebel sympathizers were proportionately disgusted because they feared it, but thought they had influence enough to prevent it.

Secretary Floyd's disappointment may be seen from this historic telegram.

WAR DEPARTMENT,

ADJUTANT-GENERAL'S OFFICE, *December* 27, 1860.

Major ANDERSON, Fort Moultrie :

Intelligence has reached here this morning that you have abandoned Fort Moultrie, spiked your guns, burned the carriages, and gone to Fort Sumter. It is not believed, because there is no order for any such movement. Explain the meaning of this report.

J. B. FLOYD,
Secretary of War.

———

CHARLESTON, *December* 27, 1860.

Hon. J. B. FLOYD, Secretary of War :

The telegram is correct. I abandoned Fort Moultrie, because I was certain that if attacked my men must have been sacrificed, and the command of the harbor lost. I spiked the guns and destroyed the carriages, to keep the guns from being used against us.

If attacked, the garrison would never have surrendered without a fight.

ROBERT ANDERSON,
Major, First Artillery.

It was this event that compelled Mr. Buchanan to change his policy within ten days after Mr. Cass left his Cabinet. He was placed under the coercion of events. Before, he had been dealing with theories ; from that time forth he found that he had to grapple with facts.

The first that confronted him was the unexpected and general outburst of patriotic sentiment in the North. As this sentiment extended also to the Northern Democracy, the President had to give his approval to Major Anderson's act.

So Mr. Floyd resigned the portfolio of war on December 31st, the day Mr. Buchanan wrote his reply to the South Carolina Commission. Mr. Cobb had previously resigned. These changes forced a reconstruction of the Cabinet. Judge Black became Secretary of State, Governor Dix took the Treasury, Holt the War Office, and Stanton became Attorney-General. Toucey and Thompson should have been dismissed. In this Book of Revelations we have an interesting despatch from Mr. Thompson.

WASHINGTON, *January*, 4, 1861.

A. N. KIMBALL, Jackson, Miss. :

No troops have been sent to Charleston, nor will be while I am a member of the Cabinet.

J. THOMPSON.

Mr. Toucey's Southern sympathies were just as pronounced as Mr. Thompson's, and if the President wished to have an efficient Cabinet he should have gotten rid of this hostile element. Black, Stanton, Dix, and Holt, were able, earnest, and patriotic men, anxious, as we now know, to uphold the honor of the government; but the truth is well known that Mr. Buchanan's feeling was expressed in his famous phrase : " After me the deluge."

To understand the policy of the administration and the acts of Anderson, we should know the orders given and received in relation to the forts in Charleston Harbor. We therefore give a *résumé* of them in order of date, omitting those that are unimportant or relate merely to matters of routine.

ADJUTANT-GENERAL'S OFFICE,
WASHINGTON, *November* 24, 1860.

Major ROBERT ANDERSON,
First Regiment Artillery, U. S. A., Commanding Fort Moultrie, Charleston, S. C. :

MAJOR.—The Secretary of War desires that you will communicate, with the least delay practicable, the present state of your command, and every thing which may relate to the condition of the work under your charge and its capabilities of defence, together with such views as you may have to suggest in respect to the same. He desires to be informed whether, in view of maintaining the troops ready for efficient action and defence, it might not be advisable to employ reliable persons, not connected with the military service, for purposes of fatigue and police.

Very respectfully, your obedient servant,

S. COOPER,
Adjutant-General.

ADJUTANT-GENERAL'S OFFICE,
November 28, 1860.

Major ROBERT ANDERSON,
U. S. A., etc., Fort Moultrie.

MAJOR.—Your letter of the 24th instant has been re-ceived and submitted to the Secretary of War. It is now under consideration, the result of which will be duly com-municated to you. In the meantime, authority has been given by the Engineer Bureau to Captain Foster to send to Castle Pinckney the engineer workmen, as suggested by you, for purposes of repairs, etc.

The Secretary desires that any communications you may have to make for the information of the Department be addressed to this office, or to the Secretary himself.

Very respectfully, your obedient servant,

S. COOPER,
Adjutant-General.

ADJUTANT-GENERAL'S OFFICE,
December 1, 1860.

Major R. ANDERSON :

SIR.—Your letter of November 28th has been received. The Secretary of War has directed Brevet Colonel Huger to repair to this city as soon as he can safely leave his post, to return there in a short time. He desires you to see Colonel Huger and confer with him, prior to his de-parture, on the matters which have been confided to each of you.

It is believed, from information thought to be reliable, that an attack will not be made on your command, and the Secretary has only to refer to his conversation with you, and to caution you that, should his convictions unhappily prove untrue, your action must be such as to be free from the charge of initiating a collision. If attacked, you are, of course, expected to defend the trust committed to you to the best of your ability.

The increase of the force under your command, however much to be desired, would, the Secretary thinks, judging from the recent excitement produced on account of an anticipated increase, as mentioned in your letter, but add to that excitement, and might lead to serious results.

S. COOPER.

FORT MOULTRIE, S. C., *December*, 11, 1860.

Memorandum of verbal instructions to Major ANDERSON, *First Artillery, commanding at Fort Moultrie, S. C.*

You are aware of the great anxiety of the Secretary of War that a collision of the troops with the people of this State shall be avoided, and of his studied determination to pursue a course with reference to the military force and forts in this harbor which shall guard against such a collision. He has therefore carefully abstained from increasing the force at this point, or taking :any measures which might add to the present excited state of the public mind, or which would throw any doubt on the confidence he feels that South Carolina will not attempt by violence, to obtain possession of the public works or interfere with their occupancy. But as the counsel and acts of rash and impulsive persons may possibly disappoint those expectations of the government, he deems it proper that you should be prepared with instructions to meet so unhappy a contingency. He has therefore directed me verbally to give you such instructions.

You are carefully to avoid every act which would needlessly tend to provoke aggression ; and for that reason you are not, without evident and imminent necessity, to take up any position which could be construed into the assumption of a hostile attitude. But you are to hold possession of the forts in this harbor, and if attacked you are to defend yourself to the last extremity. The smallness of your force will not permit you, perhaps, to occupy more one of the three forts, but an attack on or attempt to take possession of any one of them will be regarded as an act of hostility, and you may then put your command into either of them which you may deem most proper to increase its power of resistance. You are also authorized to take similar steps whenever you have tangible evidence of a design to proceed to a hostile act.

D. C. Buell,
Assistant Adjutant-General.

This is in comformity to my instructions to Major Buell.

John B. Floyd,
Secretary of War.

ADJUTANT-GENERAL'S OFFICE,

Washington, *December* 14, 1860.

Major Anderson,

First Artillery, Commanding Fort Moultrie, Charleston, S. C.

Sir :—The Secretary of War directs me to give the following answers to certain questions contained in your late letters.

If the State authorities demand any of Captain Foster's workmen on the ground of their being enrolled into the service of the State, and the subject is referred to you, you will, after fully satisfying yourself that the men are subject to enrolment, and have been properly enrolled under the laws of the United States, and of the State of South Carolina, cause them to be delivered up or suffer them to depart.

If deemed essential to the more perfect defence of the work, the levelling of the sand hills which command the fort would not, under ordinary circumstances, be considered as initiating a collision. But the delicate question of its bearing on the popular mind, in its present excited state, demands the coolest and wisest judgment.

The fact of the sand hills being private property, and, as is understood, having private residences built upon them, decides the question in the negative. The houses which might afford dangerous shelter to an enemy, being chiefly frame, could be destroyed by the heavy guns of the fort at any moment, while the fact of their being levelled in anticipation of an attack might betray distrust, and prematurely bring on a collision. Their destruction at the moment of being used as a cover for an enemy would be more fatal to the attacking force than if swept, away before their approach.

An armed body, approaching for hostile purposes, would, in all probability, either attempt a surprise or send a summons to surrender. In the former case, there can be no doubt as to the course to be pursued.

In the latter case, after refusal to surrender, and a warning to keep off, a further advance by the armed body would be initiating a collision on their part.

If no summons be made by them, their purpose should be demanded at the same time that they are warned to keep off, and their failure to answer, and further advance, would throw the responsibility upon them.

I am, etc.,

S. Cooper,
Adjutant-General.

The peculiarly infamous character of this letter will be readily perceived.

The army officers in the Charleston harbor are ordered to submit to the insolent demand of the South Carolina officials, to allow them to enroll their workmen in their militia, and also prohibiting Major Anderson from removing obstructions from before his guns.

His letter of December 21st was a protest against this ruling. On the same day that the above letter was written by the direction of the Secretary of War, the following circular was sent from Washington.

TO OUR CONSTITUENTS.

WASHINGTON, *Dec.* 14, 1860.

The argument is exhausted. All hope of relief in the Union, through the agencies of committees, Congressional legislation, or constitutional amendments, is extinguished, and we trust that the South will not be deceived by appearances or the pretence of new guaranties. In our judgment the Republicans are resolute in the purpose to grant nothing that will or ought to satisfy the South. We are satisfied the honor, safety, and independence of the Southern people require the organization of a Southern Confederacy—a result to be obtained only by separate State secession; that the primary object of each slave State ought to be its speedy and absolute separation from a union of hostile States.

Signed by :

Pugh, Clopton, Moore, Curry, Stallworth, Iverson, Underwood, Gartrell, Jackson, Jones, Crawford, Hawkins, Hindman, Jefferson Davis, A. G. Brown, Barksdale, Singleton, R. Davis, Cragie, Ruffin, Slidell, Benjamin, Loandrum, Wigfall, Hemphill, Reagan, Benham, Miles, McQueen, and Ashmore.

There can be no doubt of Floyd's knowledge of the sending of this secret circular. He was in daily consultation with many of the signers. One of the signers (Slidell) was his brother-in-law. He was busy at the time in transferring arms and munitions of war from Northern to Southern arsenals, and, finally, he knew that he was charged with being *particeps criminis* with Secretary Thompson in an embezzlement of $870,000 government funds.

December 19, 1860.

Major ROBERT ANDERSON, etc.,
Charleston, S. C.

I have just telegraphed Captain Foster to return any arms that he may have removed from Cnarleston arsenal.

J. B. FLOYD.

WAR DEPARTMENT,

WASHINGTON, December 21, 1860.

Major ANDERSON,
First Artillery, Commanding Fort Moultrie, S. C.

SIR :—In the verbal instructions communicated to you by Major Buell, you are directed to hold possession of the forts in the harbor of Charleston, and, if attacked, to defend yourself to the last extremity. Under these instructions, you might infer *that you are required to make a vain and useless sacrifice of your own life and the lives of the men under your command, upon a mere point of honor. This is far from the President's intentions. You are to exercise a sound military discretion on this subject.*

It is neither expected nor desired that you should expose your own life or that of your men in a hopeless conflict in defence of these forts. If they are invested or attacked by a force so superior that resistance would, in your judgment, be a useless waste of life, *it will be your duty to yield to necessity, and make the best terms in your power.*

This will be the conduct of an honorable, brave, and humane officer, and you will be fully justified in such action. These orders are strictly confidential, and not to be communicated even to the officers under your command without close necessity.

Very respectfully,
JOHN B. FLOYD,
Secretary of War.

This was the letter delivered by Captain John Withers, subsequently of the C. S. A. It was written the day after the secession of South Carolina, and delivered December 23, 1860. Read between the lines, it meant treason pure and simple. On receiving it, Major Anderson determined to move over to Sumter without delay.

The next was Floyd's telegram of December 27th, already given.

HEADQUARTERS OF THE ARMY.

NEW YORK, *January* 5, 1861.

Major ROBERT ANDERSON,
First Artillery, Commanding Fort Sumter.

SIR :—In accordance with the instructions of the General-in-Chief, I yesterday chartered the steamship *Star of the West* to reinforce your small garrison with two hundred well-instructed recruits from Fort Columbus, under First Lieut. C. R. Woods, Ninth Infantry, assisted by Lieuts. W. A. Webb, Fifth Infantry, and C. W. Thomas, First Infantry, and Asst. Surg. P. G. I. Ten Broeck, Medical Department, all of whom you will retain until further orders. Besides arms for the men, one hundred spare arms and all the cartridges in the arsenal on Governor's Island will be sent ; likewise three months' subsistence for the detachment, and six months' desiccated and fresh vegetables, with three or four days' fresh beef for your entire force. Further reinforcements will be sent if necessary.

Should a fire, likely to prove injurious, be opened upon any vessel bringing reinforcements or supplies, or upon tow-boats within the reach of your guns, they may be employed to silence such fire ; and you may act in like manner in case a fire is opened upon Fort Sumter itself.

The General-in-Chief desires me to communicate the fact that your conduct meets with the emphatic approbation of the highest in authority.

You are warned to be upon your guard against all telegrams, as false ones may be attempted to be passed upon you. Measures will soon be taken to enable you to correspond with the government by sea and Wilmington, N. C.

You will send to Fort Columbus by the return of the

steamer all your sick, otherwise inefficient officers and en-
listed men.   Fill up the two companies with the recruits
now sent, and muster the residue as a detachment.

I am, sir, very respecfully,

Your obedient servant, L. THOMAS.

Assistant Adjutant-General.

Not received until after the *Star of the West*
had been fired on.

WAR DEPARTMENT, *January* 10, 1861.

Major ROBERT ANDERSON,

First Artillery, Commanding at Fort Sumter, S. C.

SIR :—Your dispatches to No. 16 inclusive have been
received.   Before the receipt of that of 31st December,
announcing that the government might reinforce you at
its leisure, and that you regarded yourself safe in your
present position, some two hundred and fifty instructed
recruits had been ordered to proceed from Governor's
Island to Fort Sumter on the *Star of the West*, for the
purpose of strengthening the force under your command.
The probability is, from the current rumors of to-day,
that this vessel has been fired into by the South Carolinians, and has not been able to reach you.   To meet
all contingencies, the *Brooklyn* has been dispatched, with
instructions not to cross the bar at the harbor of Charleston, but to afford to the *Star of the West* and those on
board all the assistance they may need, and in the even
the recruits have not effected a landing at Fort Sumter
they will return to Fort Monroe.

I avail myself of the occasion to express the great satis-
faction of the government at the forbearance, discretion,
and firmness with which you have acted, amid the per-

plexing and difficult circumstances in which you have been placed. You will continue, as heretofore, to act strictly on the defensive; to avoid, by all means compatible with the safety of your command, a collision with the hostile forces by which you are surrounded. But for the movement, so promptly and brilliantly executed, by which you transferred your forces to Fort Sumter, the probability is that ere this the defencelessness of your position would have invited an attack, which, there is reason to believe, was contemplated, if not in active preparation, which must have led to the effusion of blood, that has been so happily prevented. The movement, therefore, was in every way admirable, alike for its humanity (and) patriotism, as for its soldiership.

Very respectfully, your obedient servant,

J. HOLT,
Secretary of War ad interim.

WAR DEPARTMENT, *February* 23, 1861.

Maj. ROBERT ANDERSON,
First Artillery, Commanding Fort Sumter, Charleston Harbor, S. C.

SIR :—It is proper I should state distinctly that you hold Fort Sumter as you held Fort Moultrie, under the verbal orders communicated by Major Buell, subsequently modified by instructions addressed to you from this Department, under date of the 21st of December, 1860.

In your letter to Adjutant-General Cooper, of the 16th instant, you say : "I should like to be instructed on a question which may present itself in reference to the floating-battery, viz.: What course would it be proper for me to take if, without a declaration of war or a notification of hostilities, I should see them approaching my fort with that battery? They may attempt placing it

within good distance before a declaration of hostile intention."

It is not easy to answer satisfactorily this important
question at this distance from the scene of action.   In
my letter to you of the 10th of January, I said :

" *You will continue, as heretofore, to act strictly on the
defensive*, and to avoid, by all means compatible with the
safety of your command, a collision with the hostile forces
by which you are surrounded."

The policy thus indicated must still govern your conduct.

The President is not disposed at the present moment
to change the instructions under which you have been
heretofore acting, or to occupy any other than a defensive
position.   If, however, you are convinced by sufficient
evidence that the raft of which you speak is advancing
for the purpose of making an assault upon the fort, then
you would be justified on the principle of self-defence in
not awaiting its actual arrival there, but in repelling force
by force on its approach.   If, on the other hand, you
have reason to believe that it is approaching merely to
take up a position at a good distance, should the pending
question be not amicably settled, then, unless your safety
is so clearly endangered as to render resistance an act of
necessary self-defence and protection, you will act with
that forbearance which has distinguished you heretofore
in permitting the South Carolinians to strengthen Fort
Moultrie and erect new batteries for the defence of the
harbor.   This will be but a redemption of the implied
pledge contained in my letter on behalf of the President
to Colonel Hayne, in which, when speaking of Fort Sumter, it is said :

" The attitude of that garrison, as has been often declared, is neither menacing, nor defiant, nor unfriendly.
It is acting under orders to stand strictly on the defensive,

and the government and people of South Carolina must know that they can never receive aught but shelter from its guns, unless, in the absence of all provocation, they should assault it and seek its destruction."

A dispatch received in this city a few days since from Governor Pickens, connected with the declaration on the part of those convened at Montgomery, claiming to act on behalf of South Carolina as well as the other seceded States, that the question of the possession of the forts and other public property therein had been taken from the decision of the individual States, and would probably be preceded in its settlement by negotiation with the government of the United States, has impressed the President with a belief that there will be no immediate attack on Fort Sumter, and the hope is indulged that wise and patriotic counsels may prevail and prevent it altogether.

The labors of the Peace Congress have not yet closed, and the presence of that body here adds another to the powerful motives already existing for the adoption of every measure, except in necessary self-defence, for avoiding a collision with the forces that surround you.

Very respectfully, your obedient servant,

J. Holt.

This brings the orders and correspondence down to the close of the Buchanan administration. In itself it would be incomprehensible either to the military or political student. The clue to the mystery is to be found in the correspondence between the Executive and the Hon. J. W. Hayne, the Attorney-General of South Carolina.

While Mr. Crittenden was devising compromises and Mr. Taylor and his confreres were getting up peace conventions, Mr. Hayne came to Washington to serve, as it were, a legal process on the government. He tendered payment on the part of his State for all government property in the borders of South Carolina, and in case the United States government did not see fit to accept his offer, he gave notice, on the part of his free and sovereign State, of its intention to act by forcible entry and detainer. Singularly enough, the President answered this piece of political impertinence by a long chop-logic letter through Mr. Holt, his Secretary of War.

Driven from his non-intervention standpoint by the outburst of patriotic feeling that followed the occupation of Sumter, Mr. Buchanan had to assume the position, in a message he sent to Congress on the 8th of January, 1861, that he was bound to hold the forts as public property.

Seeing that he claimed for his government no right of sovereignty, but only a property right, founded on purchase and relinquishment, South Carolina adroitly came forward with her claim of eminent domain and national sovereignty.

No one cares for this controversy now, but it throws a strong light on the character of the Old Public Functionary, and explains many apparent inconsistencies.

Up to the time of his election to the Presidency, Mr. Buchanan had been very generally considered a man of ability his speeches and State papers were creditable, if not brilliant; yet as an executive officer in a great crisis he was an evident failure. It seems to me that his failure resulted from a misunderstanding of the philosophy of history, which caused him to misapprehend the first principles of national growth. He seemed to think that the Contract Socialè was something more than an illustrative theory ; that nations could be formed by agreement, held together by paper constitutions or dissolved by mutual consent. He seemed to think that the constitution made the American Nation and was not rather the expression of the *lex non scripta* of our national life. He did not seem to understand the principle of the unification of races, and that, with us at least the cohesive principle was as strong as reason habit, pride, self-interest, and love of liberty could make it. The deluge overtook him and in its waves his political reputation perished.

If the publication of the Rebellion record:

give us no positively new information in relation to the two expeditions sent to the relief of Sumter, it will at least settle some disputed points.

Judge Black has recently asserted that Lieutenant-General Scott was responsible for the failure of these expeditions. Yet it appears from the record that the first attempt, at least, was suggested by the Lieutenant-General. On December 28, 1860, Scott wrote to the Secretary of War, requesting : first, that Sumter should not be given up ; second, that it be reinforced and provisioned ; and, third, that two armed vessels should be sent to support the fort.

As Mr. Floyd resigned the next day, General Scott wrote to the President direct to the same effect. On the 31st of December he sent an order to Colonel Dimick, at Fort Monroe, to send four companies to Sumter by the sloop-of-war *Brooklyn*.

The President was subsequently persuaded to substitute a merchant steamer, the *Star of the West*, for the *Brooklyn*.

Unfortunately the garrison of Sumter was not notified of its coming, and was taken completely by surprise when the Morris Island batteries opened fire. Before they got ready to fight the vessel had turned back. This was on January 9th. When the fort was occupied fourteen days before, it must be remembered that it was in the hands of Captain Foster's workmen, and in a very unfinished state. It was literally filled with construction material and debris. The parade was covered with their frame workshops. The gorge was open ; the embrasures boarded up loosely with inch plank ; only the lighter guns were mounted ; the heavy guns were not mounted before the fifteenth, as stated by General Doubleday in his personal reminiscences of Moultrie and Sumter. The distance from Sumter to the Star of the West battery was 2,800 yards. At that distance any of the guns then mounted at Sumter would have been ineffective. The South Carolina authorities were notified of the departure and mission of the *Star of the West* by Mr. Thompson, the Secretary of the Interior, who learned the purpose of the President at a Cabinet meeting, the proceedings of which were declared confidential.

Captain Ward, of the navy, who commanded the receiving ship *North Carolina* in New York harbor, in the winter of 1861, proposed during the month of February to relieve fort Sumter by using four or more small coast survey steamers. Mr. Cameron, in the synopsis of the various plans for the relief of Sumter, which he laid before President Lincoln, on March 15, 1861, says that this plan met with General Scott's concurrence, but that the late President would not allow the attempt to be made (" Rebellion Records," vol. i, p. 197).   Subsequently it is stated that Captain Ward afterward abandoned his plan, after consultation with General Scott.   Yet on the 20th of February, the Lieutenant-General wrote to Colonel H. L. Scott, his A. D. C., in New York City, directing him to prepare the expedition as soon as Captain Ward could get his squadron ready.   Judge Black, then Secretary of State, is authority for the statement that President Buchanan withdrew his assent to Captain Ward's expedition upon General Scott's advice.

On the 16th of January, 1861, Judge Black addressed a letter to the Lieut.-General, urging a renewed attempt to reinforce Major Anderson.   General Scott never answered that letter, and the probabilities are that he had even then formed the opinion that any further attempt to relieve Sumter would be unadvisable.   It is very improbable that the *Star of the West* was substituted for the *Brooklyn* upon his advice, in view of his earnest recommendation, already quoted, made upon December 28, 1860, that two armed vessels be sent to the support of Fort Sumter.

But there is, I think, no doubt that he was opposed to all attempts to relieve the garrison of Sumter by sea.

General Scott, in answer to a question addressed to him by Mr. Lincoln, on the 12th of April, replied.

"I should need a fleet of war vessels and transports which, in the scattered disposition of the navy (as understood), could not be collected in less than four months : 5,000 additional regular troops, and 20,000 volunteers ; that is, a force sufficient to take all the batteries, both in the harbor (including Fort Moultrie) as well as in the approach or outer bay. To raise, organize, and discipline such an army (not to speak of necessary legislation by Congress, not now in session) would require from six to eight months. As a practical military question the time for succoring Fort Sumter with any means at hand had passed away nearly a month ago. Since then a surrender under assault or from starvation has been merely a question of time."

What is still more conclusive is the evidence contained in the " Rebellion Records," of the truth of the assertions of Mr. Welles and Mr. Montgomery Blair : that Mr. William H. Seward and Lieut.-General Scott obtained the order from President Lincoln which detached the *Powhatan* from Mr. Fox's relief expedition to Sumter. First we have the letter of Mr. Lincoln (p. 406, " Rebellion Records ") assuming the responsibility for relieving Captain Mercer and of placing Lieutenant D. D. Porter in command of the *Powhatan*. Next we have this letter of Mr. Secretary Welles' " young captain named Meigs."

QUARTERMASTER-GENERAL'S OFFICE,
WASHINGTON, D. C., *February* 27, 1865.

Bvt. Brig. Gen. E. D. TOWNSEND,
Assistant Adjutant-General, War Department.

MY DEAR GENERAL:—The Navy Department has no copy of the instructions to D. D. Porter and other naval officers under which they co-operated with the expedition of April 1861, to reinforce Fort Pickens.

The President has none, and they have applied to me. My copies, I think, I placed in Hartsuff's hands. He was adjutant of the expedition.

Please forward the enclosed note to him, and if you have copies, let me have, for the Navy Department, a copy of the President's order to Porter, and to other naval officers. Also of the order to Colonel Brown, which required all naval officers to aid him.

General Scott knew of the expedition and its orders ; and you were acting confidentially with him and may have had custody of those orders, which were kept secret even from the Secretaries of War and Navy, I believe.

Yours truly,
M. C. MEIGS,
Quartermaster-General, Brevet Major-General.

It is hard to understand why Gen. Scott sanctioned the transfer of the *Powhatan* from the Sumter to the Pickens expedition without the knowledge of either the Secretary of War or the Secretary of the Navy. He was a great soldier, a cultivated gentleman, the soul of honor, and a true patriot. Yet the fact seems indisputable. It may be that he knew he could not save Fort Sumter, and hoped to save Fort Pickens at the sacrifice of the other. A general may give up an outpost, like a chess-player offering a gambit pawn, but, as before remarked, the mystery in this case is that he acted without the knowledge of the heads of departments. The following letter from Gen. Meigs fully explains his connection with the Pickens expedition.

WASHINGTON, *Oct.* 31, 1881.

Lt. Col. THOMAS M. ANDERSON,
     9th Infantry, Fort McKinney, Wyo. Ter.

MY DEAR SIR :—I have not time to reply fully to your questions about Pickens. Something on the subject from me you will find in Scott's two volumes of the "Records of the Rebellion " thus far published.

I may say that Mr. Seward took me to see President Lincoln, saying that he understood that some officers of higher rank than myself were indisposed to advise active measures to relieve posts in danger. That he had nothing to say as to how I should speak to Mr. Lincoln ; he wished me to answer any questions put to me according to my best belief and knowledge.

Mr. Lincoln asked whether Sumter could be relieved. I said that was a matter for the navy. It must be done by ships. That there might be difference of opinion on such a subject, but that I was sure I could find him young naval officers then in Washington, who would gladly, if authorized, undertake to attempt it.

He then dropped the subject, and I heard no more of Sumter till at Santa Rosa Island I saw extracts from newspapers, mutilated slips sent to Fort Pickens by General Bragg, announcing its surrender as a military necessity.

The subject of Pickens was taken up. I had passed it going out of Pensacola Harbor in November, 1860, and was familiar with the maps and plans of the position in the engineer office.

Could Fort Pickens be reinforced? Yes, if done in time. The embrasures are a few feet only above the bottom of the ditch, and a *coup-de-main* with loss of a few men, could, I believed, carry it against the very insufficient garrison under Slemmer.

How can it be done? Send a ship of war immediately under sealed orders to enter the harbor and prevent boat expeditions crossing from Pensacola to Santa Rosa Island. For this purpose I recommended, for reasons which I stated fully, and which were derived from his history, Lieut. David Porter, now Admiral Porter. I also said Providence supplies the man and the means. Porter I had seen within a day or so in Washington, and I learned by the newspapers that the *Powhatan* had just returned from a foreign cruise. If she could cross the Atlantic she could at once go to Pickens.

Send as soon as possible troops and supplies in a

transport steamer to land and reinforce the garrison of Pickens.

The *Powhatan* will prevent the boat expedition, which, I said, might be at that moment (it was after dark) under weigh ; if she got in, the others would relieve the fortress. The island is fitted with longitudinal sand ridges, which would protect troops and stores landed on the beach east of the fort and out of the range of the rebel batteries in their approach to Pickens.

The President said he would perhaps send for me again. I urged that the strictest secrecy was indispensable, as it was known that telegrams had communicated information to the Southern leaders.

I had no suspicion of anybody in high station, but the ordinary business of the executive departments brings every paper under the eye of more than one person. A secretary cannot take care of the papers he signs or acts upon. They are too many, and clerks and others are necessary to perform the mere physical labor of caring for records and dispatching and filing official papers. I believe that it was suggested afterward by Porter that the telegraph wires around Washington ought all to be cut.

The President sent for me again on a Saturday evening or a Sunday morning, and directed that Colonel Keyes, Military Secretary to General Scott, and myself should draw up a project for the relief of Pickens, submit it to General Scott, and do this by, I think, 2 P. M. of Sunday.

We went to the engineer office, to which, though closed, I had access, got out the plans of Santa Rosa and of Pensacola Harbor, prepared our project, took it to General Scott, who, after discussion, approved it as it stood, except the provision authorizing the commander of the expedition to declare martial law on the Gulf Coast, especially at Key West. This he thought illegal. Mr. Seward came in ; we discussed it ; I urged its legality and necessity. The Constitution was examined again, and Mr. Seward said that was authority enough for him, and we should have power to declare martial law.

He said he wished me to go with the expedition, and he suggested that I should be given rank to command it. General Scott told him that all the power of the President then could not make a captain a major even, which I knew well enough. I told Mr. Seward that I was in this contest and ready to go with my present rank or with none at all.

General Scott was earnest and fully approved. He objected to our proposition to take a mounted battery of artillery then in Washington, as taking away all his strength in this city. I said : " General, if this comes to war you will want not a battery of artillery here, but a large force, and the regular army will be nothing ; it will be the yeomanry of the country that will come to defend Washington." He then consented.

The force taken has been published. Porter had orders, drawn up by myself and Keyes, signed by the President's own hand, to take the *Powhatan.* Telegram to New York Navy Yard, and letter to her then commander from the President, ordered her to be dispatched under Porter's command at the earliest possible moment and under sealed orders, her destination unknown to her then commander or crew, or to the officers at the navy yard.

Major Harvey Brown was ordered to command the troops which were gathered at New York and dispatched in the steamer *Atlantic*, which I accompanied.

The rest is history.

She was followed by the *Illinois*, with other troops.

I heard no one hint any doubt of the good faith of any executive officer or of General Scott. He entered heartily into the project, and was kind and cordial to the authors. I think he recognized the importance of absolute secrecy for protection against information which might leak out if the project was known to any but those who were engaged in it.

I think that Mr. Lincoln, Mr. Seward, General Scott, Harvey Brown, after he received his orders, Keyes, Lieut. David Porter, and myself were the only persons who knew the destination of the troops, of the *Powhatan*, or of the *Atlantic*, until the steamers *Powhatan* and *Atlantic* reached Santa Rosa.

The *Powhatan* was delayed in New York, and sailed only an hour or two before the *Atlantic*, and the latter, being the faster vessel, arrived at least a day before the *Powhatan*, and the troops were in Pickens before the *Powhatan* hove in sight. Then, at request of Harvey Brown, I met the *Powhatan* with difficulty, and only by laying the ship I was on athwart her bows, stopped her and explained to Porter that the fort being reinforced it would be a crime to expose his ship and crew to injury by attempting to enter the harbor.

The secrecy was to prevent leaks from whatever source, and not from doubt of the loyalty and fidelity of any officer of high position.

If you wish to keep any project secret, tell it to nobody, and to those to be engaged in it tell only so much as will direct their movements till it is necessary to tell more.

All the orders for the expedition were drawn up by Keyes and myself, and they were signed in effect exactly as we advised.

I knew of no attempt to relieve Sumter. It appeared afterward that Naval Secretary Welles destined the *Powhatan* for Sumter. He had not, I believe, perfected his plan at the time I suggested her use for Pickens, for when we got to New York, instead of finding her ready to sail, we found her crew detached and the ship partially, at least, dismantled, so that it took some days of active, earnest work to get a crew on board and make her ready to sail.

When I first spoke with the President on her use, I had just seen in the day's papers her arrival in New York reported, and I supposed she could start as soon as ordered.

I do not believe that the *Powhatan* was changed from the Sumter to the Pickens expedition. I believe that the first order was Mr. Lincoln's, giving her to Porter and Pickens, and that in ignorance of this order, she was destined by the Navy Department to Sumter. But Mr. Lincoln's sign-manual to Porter's orders to take command, and to Captain Mercer's orders to resign command, overruled the orders of the Secretary of the Navy, which, I believe, were received while Porter and Foote, who was then in command of the Brooklyn Navy Yard, were straining every nerve to refit her for a destination unknown to all navy officers and the Navy Department, except Porter.

He called me to Brooklyn, finding the case blocked, and I showed Captains Mercer and Foote the sign-manual of the President ; told them that the Secretary of the Navy and the Secretary of War knew nothing of this, and asked which they would obey, the President or his Secretary. They concluded to obey the President's order exhibited to them.

The President, therefore, if he changed at all the destination of the *Powhatan*, did it after he had signed orders sending her to Pickens.

I had no occasion to discuss the question of saving or sacrificing Sumter as against Pickens. After advising the President that I could find him naval officers who would be glad to attempt the relief of Sumter, that fortress was not again mentioned in my presence.

I had no apprehension from, and I heard none expressed of, spies in high places. My object was to avoid leakage, which is sure to occur in a vessel of too many joints or parts, and I urged that nobody know what we intended to do, except those who directed and controlled, and the orders to the *Atlantic* were to sail in a certain direction from New York, and at a certain distance open an order which directed only the next stage of the voyage, etc., etc.

General Scott's feelings and inclinations have been much discussed. All I saw of him during his life was hearty, true loyalty, and fidelity to his oath as an officer of the army of the United States.

I believe I have answered, as fully as I can without searching documents for dates, all your questions.

I remain, respectfully, your obedient servant,

M. C. MEIGS,

Quartermaster-General, Bvt. Major-General, U. S. A.

There is also a letter from General Meigs to Mr. Seward, too long to quote, which contains this felicitation, of the success of their conspiracy by which the naval expedition to Sumter was deliberately ruined :

" Your dispatch arrived as I was on my way to the *Atlantic*, just before the hour at which she was to sail, and two or three hours after that appointed for the *Powhatan*. *When the arrow has sped from the bow it may glance aside, but who shall reclaim it before its flight is finished?* " (P. 369.)

This letter was written at sea, yet Captain Meigs evidently feared that either the Secretary of War or the Secretary of the Navy might get intelligence of the orders sent to the *Powhatan* without their knowledge, and still reclaim her even in her flight.

In the long letter of instructions from General Scott to Colonel Harvey Brown, commanding the Pickens expedition, approved by the President, and which was supplemented by an endorsement by Mr. Lincoln, directing all officers of the army and navy to aid the expedition, there is no word to warn the President that the *Powhatan* was to be used for the purpose of the Pickens expedition.

As the *Powhatan* had on board all the troops intended to reinforce Sumter, and all the barges provided for the landing of both soldiers and supplies, when she was detached, of course the expedition failed.

It is only fair to say that Pickens was saved if Sumter was sacrificed.[1]

The most singular fact in this connection is that both General Scott and General Totten (chief of engineers) had been asserting that neither Sumter nor Pickens could be saved.

An account of the siege and fall of Fort Sumter may be very briefly given. It is a matter of very little military importance, its significance being altogether political. Only such important points in the oft-repeated story will be referred to, as may be necessary for a better understanding of the great drama of Rebellion, of which it was the prelude.

Major Anderson had warned his government that the people of South Carolina intended to take forcible possession of the forts in Charleston Harbor as soon as the State convention adopted the ordinance of secession. He had

---

[1] The opinions of the army and navy officers laid before President Lincoln, as given in the " Rebellion Record," vol. i, p. 196, *et sequentia*, may be summarized as follows :

Gen. Scott and Gen. Totten did not think that Fort Sumter could be relieved with the means they had or were likely to get.

Gen. Anderson thought such an enterprise would require 20,000 men. Gen. Seymour, his second in command, thought the attempt would result in a siege as formidable and protracted as that of Sebastopol.

Lieut. Synder, Eng. Corp.: four thousand men and four vessels of war.

Lieut. R. K. Mead, Eng. Corp.: 5,000 men, supported by gun-boats.

Dr. S. W. Crawford (afterward General) : 4,000 men, supported by the navy.

Lieut. (afterward General) J. C. Davis : 3,000 men and six war vessels.

reason to believe this from the open declaration of their highest State officials, and their military preparations all over those States. He regarded the proclamation of the ordinance of secession on December 20th, as an open act of rebellion, and, six days after, moved to the safer position on the island of Sumter. To give the fullest possible confirmation to his belief, the South Carolina militia took possession of Fort Moultrie and Castle Pinckney the next day. On the 30th they seized the United States arsenal in Charleston, entering it by escalade. In point of fact they had had a guard over it for two weeks, under the poor pretext, before referred to, that their slaves might take it. They claimed that Major Anderson's change of base was an act of war. Yet they had been preparing for war and levying war for months.

They began erecting batteries about Sumter within twenty-four hours of its occupation.

Lieut. Theodore Talbot, 1st Art.: 3,000 men and navy.

Capt. (afterward Gen.) A. Doubleday : 10,000 men and navy.

Captain (afterward Gen.) Foster : 6,000 regulars, or 20,000 volunteers to take them ; 10,000 regulars or 30,000 volunteers to hold them.

Commodore Stringham agreed with Foster. As Foster had once belonged to the Coast Survey, he probably knew more about the question than all the rest put together.

Gen Geo. B. McClellan, then in Cincinnati, told the writer, the day the rebel guns opened on Sumter, that that fort was utterly indefensible, and would not hold out forty-eight hours. This was somewhat surprising, as an officer of engineers, now a general in the army, had, on the evening before, explained to a set of gratified listeners, that Fort Sumter was impregnable.

They fired into the *Star of the West* on January 9, 1861. On the 11th the governor of South Carolina demanded the surrender of the fort. On the first of March the Confederate government assumed control of the forces in Charleston Harbor. General Beauregard assumed command on the 3d, and on the same day the schooner *Rhoda H. Shannon* was fired on by the Confederate batteries, this being their first overt act of war.

Major Anderson never feared the South Carolina militia ; as long as they were his only opponents he assured his government that he was perfectly secure in his position.

But when the Confederate authorities took charge of the siege operations against him, they soon made such a show of strength and energy that he discovered his mistake, and frankly avowed it. As soon as he could do so, he informed the War Department, not only of the difficulty of holding the fort, but of the serious obstacles that would have to be overcome in effecting its relief.

It was on the 12th of March, 1861, that the so-called Confederate Commissioners arrived in Washington, and asked permission to call on the President, and present their credentials as the embassadors of a foreign power. This was ot course declined, but they were nevertheless allowed to remain in Washington until they voluntarily left, after the sailing of the second Sumter expedition on the 10th of April.

The Rebellion records give us the despatches and letters these gentlemen and other confederates in political crime were allowed to send from Washington in the last days of Mr. Buchanan's, and in the early days of Mr. Lincoln's administration. We will give a few samples.

Iolt succeeds Floyd. It means war. Cut off supplies from Anderson and take Sumter soon as possible.

Louis T. Wigfall.

(A United States Senator drawing pay from the United States Government.)

President's reply : "*Brooklyn* not for South Carolina. On errand of mercy and relief.

"John Tyler."

This shows that Mr. Buchanan was himself responsible for the substitution of the *Star of the West* for the *Brooklyn*.

Washington, *January* 8, 1861.

The *Star of the West* sailed from New York on Sunday with government troops and provisions. It is said her destination is Charleston. If so; she may be hourly expected off the harbor.

Louis T. Wigfall.

The fact that troops were on board was supposed to be a profound state secret.

But there seemed to be no secrets. Even after Mr. Lincoln's inauguration, despatch after despatch was sent from Washington to the Confederate authorities, in relation to the movement of troops and of vessels of war, giving information also as to all that went on in Cabinet meetings : that the vote in Mr. Lincoln's Cabinet stood six to one in favor of withdrawing Major Anderson's command from Sumter ; that no faith could be put in Seward's promise, no faith in the administration ; and finally, on the 9th of April, we have Mr. Commissioner Crawford's final despatch : "That diplomacy had failed. The sword must now preserve our independence."

But the most interesting despatch is this :

WASHINGTON, *April* 6, 1861.
Hon. A. G. MAGRATH, *Charleston, S. C.*
Positively determined not to withdraw Anderson. Supplies go immediately ; supported by naval force under Stringham, if their landing be resisted.
(Signed), A FRIEND.

This "Friend" turned out to be James E. Harvey, who subsequently found means to have himself appointed Minister to Portugal.

Certainly there is no other government that

would have allowed such traitors to have remained at large in its capital for a single day.

But the strangest thing in this strange, eventful history, was the course taken by the Secretary of State. For years Mr. William H. Seward had been the political leader of Abolitionism; he spoke of the antagonism between freedom and slavery as the *irrepressible conflict*, and reiterated Mr. Garrison's famous saying, that there is a "higher law than the Constitution," in a debate on the floor of the Senate. Yet no sooner had he in his official capacity declined to receive and recognize Messrs. Crawford, Roman, and Forsyth, in their diplomatic capacity, than he entered into a private correspondence and negotiation with them. The Secretary seemed to be struck with judicial blindness, and to be filled with hopes as vain as those of the Bourbons that their white flag will once again wave over fair France. He yielded to the delusion that the rebel States could be induced to revoke their ordinances of secession; give up a contest he himself had declared to be irrepressible, and return peacefully to the Union. To effect this purpose, he promised that the garrison of Sumter should be withdrawn.

At the very time the Secretary of State was entering upon these ways that were dark and tricks that were vain, Mr. Cameron, the Secretary of War, laid before Mr. Lincoln and his Cabinet a paper, already referred to, giving the opinions of many prominent naval and army officers, as to the expediency and possibility of relieving Sumter, and their suggestions as to how this purpose could be best effected in case that course should be determined on. By far the greatest number consulted gave their opinion that the attempt should not be made with the means then at the government's disposal. With the sole exception of the Hon. Montgomery Blair, the members of the President's Cabinet advised him to give up any purpose of relieving Fort Sumter, and to withdraw the garrison before the 15th of April, when its supply of subsistence would be exhausted.

From a merely military point of view, this advice would have been sound, but Mr. Lincoln and Mr. Blair judged more wisely that it would be better to sacrifice the garrison of Sumter for political effect. As nearly all his military advisers had given their reasons for believing that Fort Sumter could not be relieved by less than an army of twenty thousand men and a powerful fleet, the President must have known that his expedition of two hundred men, mostly

recruits, and the absurd naval force, under Mr.
Fox, would fail as it did fail.   But the expedition was sent in accordance with a generous
public sentiment, and with the knowledge that
it would compel the rebels to strike the first
blow.   If the last man in the garrison of Sumter had perished, it would have been a cheap
price to pay for the magnificent outburst of
patriotism that followed.   Indeed it might have
been better if they had.

If the example of no surrender had been set
there, we would have had fewer capitulations to
armed rebels afterward.

When Mr. Seward found that Mr. Lincoln
had determined to reinforce both Sumter and
Pickens, he notified the rebel Commissioners of
the fact, and induced the President to send formal notice to the authorities at Charleston.
This note was delivered on the night of April
8, 1861, to General Beauregard and Governor
Pickens.   Then, too, the extraordinary plot was
carried out, by which the *Powhatan* was detached from the Sumter expedition and sent to
Florida.   The order was sent on board of her
after she was steaming down the harbor and
just passing Staten Island.

Mr. Gideon Welles, in his reminiscences, is
very severe in his condemnation of the decep-

tion Mr. Seward practised in this matter both on the Secretaries of War and the Navy. He asserts that it was prompted by his determination to make good his promise to the rebel Commissioners, that Sumter should be evacuated. Mr. Blair (the Secretary of the Interior), in a letter published in Mr. Welles' reminiscences (p. 66), says :

" Mr. Seward had two objects in detaching this vessel (the *Powhatan*).

" 1st.—It defeated the relief of Fort Sumter which he was pledged to surrender.

" 2d.—Fort Pickens could be claimed as having been saved by an expedition conceived and carried into execution under his orders, and so, though he would by this movement abandon his method of meeting exactions with concessions, and violence with peace, he would signalize his abandonment of his peace policy by a success in administering the force policy, as would put himself *per saltum* at the head of his opponents."

It has been asserted that General Scott was opposed to the relief of Sumter from his southern sympathies, and that General Anderson was lukewarm in its defence for the same reason.

These charges against those distinguished officers can be examined together.

One of the lieut.-general's avowed reasons
for not approving attempts for the relief of
Sumter was, that Major Anderson had never
asked for reinforcements after he occupied that
post. This was not only true, but that officer
had written to the adjutant-general on the 6th
of January, that he would not ask for reinforcements, because he did not know what the ulteri-
or designs of the government were, and for
the further reason that from that time on he
could only be relieved by a powerful fleet.

His first report read to Mr. Lincoln was this:
" I confess that I would not be willing to risk
my reputation on an attempt to throw reinforcements into this harbor within the time for our
relief rendered necessary by the limited supply
of our provisions, and with a view of holding
possession of the same, with a force of less than
twenty thousand good and well-disciplined
men."

At this time General Scott and Major Anderson had probably a perfect understanding and
agreement about the Sumter problem. They
had long been intimate personal friends. Major
Anderson's eldest brother, who died as our first
minister to Columbia, had been a classmate
with Scott at William and Mary's College in
Virginia. Anderson himself had been several

times on the staff of the old chief. At the battle of Moleno del Rey in Mexico, Scott had to send his friend on a most desperate attack, in which he received five wounds and nearly lost his life. After that General Scott always showed the greatest sympathy and regard for him. Moreover Major Anderson had married a daughter of General Clinch, an old compatriot of Scott's. They were both border State men, and had, in fine, a remarkable concordance in sympathies and opinions.

It is important to state these facts in this connection, because if General Scott afterward apparently abandoned one of his most cherished friends to his fate, he must evidently have been influenced by some powerful consideration.

It will be remembered that in his first letter from Moultrie, Major Anderson had urged the occupation in force of Castle Pinckney and Forts Sumter and Moultrie. The military reason for this is obvious. Castle Pinckney could command and overawe Charleston so long as Sumter and Moultrie kept open its communication with the sea.

In Major Anderson's opinion all three forts or none should have been held.

With the rest of the harbor held by an enemy, Fort Sumter was useless and untenable. At a time of great political excitement, he wrote of making the fort impregnable, but General Scott knew better, and every officer consulted by the Secretary of War put himself on record to the contrary. General Anderson was a good artillery officer, the author or compiler of the artillery text-books we were using at that time, and he really knew better. He told the writer that he knew his garrison was being sacrificed to a political necessity, and that *therefore* he did not wish another man to be sent to him. During the months of January and February all the cotton States seceded, and Anderson knew perfectly well that they could surround him with an army of twenty thousand men. He has also been censured by so-called soldiers and plaintive patriots for not opening fire when the rebels began placing batteries around him.

The writer once asked him why he did not open fire when he saw the first shovelful of earth turned at Cummings' Point. He replied, in effect, that he had three reasons : First, he was not perfectly secure against escalade until the middle of January ; secondly, he had orders to await attack ; and, thirdly, that he had not been educated to consider the Secretary of War a traitor (referring to Floyd).

I have before said that the majority of Mr.

Buchanan's reconstructed Cabinet were able and patriotic men. Why was it that Major Anderson's orders were not changed under their administration? They were temporizing to save the border States. We know now that they were attempting a vain thing. It was not thought so then. The hopeful put faith in peace conventions and Crittenden compromises.

If Major Anderson had opened fire on the Carolina militia on the 27th of December, let us speculate for a moment on the probable results.

Would Mr. Buchanan have called out the military strength of the nation to have sustained him?

It is certain he would not. Then, no matter what the fate of Sumter, which, indeed, would have been as dust in the balance, the obvious result would have been that Mr. Lincoln could only have gone to Washington like Cromwell, at the head of his Covenanters. What a sad precedent would this have been? What a loss of prestige? What a sacrifice of moral power?

The State of Kentucky, instead of remaining loyal, would have been actively hostile, and the war would have opened at once on the Ohio and the Potomac.

In that event thousands of hardy troops that hastened to the defence of the national capital would, in the first instance, have had to guard their own borders. McClellan and Rosecrantz could not have invaded Western Virginia if rebel camp-fires had been lighted on the hills back of Covington. The ultimate result might have been the same, but the final triumph would have been more difficult and long deferred.

General Anderson's course at Sumter, and his popularity as a Kentuckian, turned the wavering sentiment in that State in favor of the the Union. It was in recognition of this fact that Mr. Lincoln, himself a Kentuckian, sent General Anderson there as the first department commander.

These considerations had also great influence with General Scott. But when Judge Black was urging him, much too late, to send reinforcements to Sumter, he was also possessed with the idea that the rebels had formed a plot to seize Washington City just before Mr. Lincoln's inauguration. Our navy was scattered over the four quarters of the globe, and our little army was, for the most part, stationed in insignificant fragments on our most distant frontiers. To collect a few reliable regulars in Washington was his first and greatest care.

Yet why did he not reinforce Sumter after the capital was secured ?

I can also answer this question.

I once heard General Scott and General Anderson discuss the Sumter problem in New York City, during the siege of Fort Wagner by General Gilmore. Some one asked General Anderson as to the best way of taking Sumter. He replied : " Take Charleston." General Scott then said : " Yes, Robert, that is the way to take the Charleston forts. To attack Sumter from the sea, is taking hold of the wrong end of the poker."

There are only two other points in connection with this famous siege that require notice.

Mr. Blair, in his published letter, already referred to, makes this statement :

" General Anderson had made preparations to defend it (Sumter), but left his barracks standing, to be fired at the first shot, instead of pulling them down and taking to his casemates *as he certainly would have done* if he had not been authoritatively told that the fort was to be evacuated as soon as the small supply of provisions on hand had been consumed."

In this connection I beg leave to quote from

a letter written to me by General Truman Seymour on this subject. Seymour commanded one
of the companies of artillery in Sumter, and was
General Anderson's room-mate during the siege.

" General Anderson did not take down ' the
wooden barracks ' at Sumter—the necessity for
which was so sagely suggested by Mr. Blair,—
because there were none to take down ! The
three barracks were permanent structures of
brick, three stories high, and built solidly against
the faces of the casemates ; they were constructed by the engineers to be fire-proof, and
were supposed so to be : not a member of the
garrison ever suspected they would or could be
consumed as they were. The floors were of
brick arches upon iron beams, overlaid by a
board floor ; the sash and casings of windows
were of wood, and the slate roofing was fastened
to board sheathing. The burning of these
buildings was only a temporary inconvenience ;
after the dense smoke had been blown off
there was no longer any point worthy of notice in
connection with them. The burning of the gates
to the fort could easily have been made good
by the rubbish near it. When Sumter was occupied, the parade was crowded with wooden
sheds, shops, etc., all of which were soon cleared
away.

" The point made by Mr. Blair is too absurd to be worthy even of refutation ; he should have known better (as a graduate of West Point) than to have raised it.

" General Anderson never had the slightest suggestion from the government, or from any member of it, that the command would be withdrawn. He would doubtless have felt profoundly humiliated at any such acknowledgment of weakness—so would any of the officers there."

Strange as it may seem, General Seymour was mistaken in supposing that his commanding officer had never received an intimation that the garrison of Sumter would be withdrawn. On the 25th of March Mr. Lamon, Mr. Lincoln's private secretary, went to Sumter and told Major Anderson that in a few days his command would probably be transferred to another fort. He also made the same communication to Governor Pickens. It shows how closely Anderson kept his counsel, when he never communicated this intelligence to his second in command. This gave rise to a very strange episode.[1]

[1] The Chew Memorandum, presented to Gov. Pickens and Gen. Beauregard by Lieut. Talbot and Robert S. Chew, Esq., was as follows :

" I am directed by the President of the United States to notify you to expect an attempt will be made to supply Fort Sumter with provisions only, and that if such an attempt be not resisted, no effort

The next day General Beauregard wrote Major Anderson a very friendly personal note, congratulating him on his prospective removal, offering to give him every assistance possible, but saying finally that he would only require of him his statement on honor, that he had not mined the fort. ("Rebellion Records," vol. i, p. 222.) Anderson replied: * * * " I must state most distinctly, that if I can only be permitted to leave on the pledge you mention, I shall never, so help me, God, leave this fort alive." • (*Ibid.*)

There was a rumor that Fort Sumter was to be blown up by the Yankees when they left it.

Curiously enough, Captain Foster had written to the Chief of Engineers, December 19, 1860, "that he proposed to connect a powerful Daniel's battery with the magazine at Sumter, by means of wires stretched across under water to Fort Moultrie, and to blow up Sumter if taken by an armed force."

This, of course, was before that fort was occupied by our people. But how did the rebels get the rumor? Evidently there was a leaky vessel in the Engineer Department.

---

to throw in men, arms, or ammunition will be made without further notice, or in case of an attack on the fort.

" April 8, 1861."

This memorandum was not communicated to Major Anderson, and the *Powhatan*, with the troops, was secretly detached.

It may be inferred from General Seymour's letter that he believed that the fort could have been held longer ; Captain Foster, in his report of the siege, also says as much.

This is undoubtedly true.   By putting the garrison on starvation rations of pork, the fort could probably have been held for a week or ten days longer.   But what would have been gained by this delay ?   There were eighty men (only thirty-five of whom were skilled artillerists) holding a sea-coast fort against eight thousand.   Apart from the moral effect, the only purpose in delay would have been to have kept this many men a little longer from the Northern frontier.   This would have been a sufficient reason, and the sacrifice would have been made, had the government ever intimated its desire that it should be made.

The Administration of Mr. Lincoln showed nothing but doubt and vacillation in regard to the Sumter question, up to the time of the fall of the fort.

Evidently all it cared for was a show of force on the part of the garrison, and a proof of aggression on the part of the rebels.

This is unquestionably so, or they would not have greeted the defenders of Sumter with thanks and approval.

The truth is, I believe, that they intended to sacrifice them for moral effect, and both the Administration and the nation were happy to see them get off with their lives.

From February 23d to April 4th, no orders were sent from the War Department to Fort Sumter. Its commanding officer was thrown on his own resources, left to his own devices, yet hampered by the old order *not to fire unless attacked.* At last, however, Secretary Cameron sent the following autograph letter :

WAR DEPARTMENT.

WASHINGTON, D. C., *April* 4, 1861.

Major ROBERT ANDERSON, U. S. Army.

SIR :   Your letter of the 1st instant occasioned some anxiety to the President.

On the information of Captain Fox, he had supposed you could hold out till the 15th instant without any great inconvenience, and had prepared an expedition to relieve you before that period.

Hoping still that you will be able to sustain yourself till the 11th or 12th instant, the expedition will go forward ; and, finding your flag flying will attempt to provision you ; and, in case the effort is resisted, will endeavor also to reinforce you.

You will therefore hold out, if possible, till the arrival of the expedition.

It is not, however, the intention of the President to subject your command to any *danger or hardship beyond what, in your judgment, would be usual in military life ;* and he has entire confidence that you will act as becomes a patriot and soldier under all circumstances.

Whenever, if at all, in your judgment, to save yourself and command, *a capitulation becomes a necessity, you are authorized to make it.*

SIMON CAMERON,
Secretary of War.

The answer to the above letter was intercepted by the Confederates and sent to Montgomery. It never reached Washington until it went there with the Confederate archives. It was accompanied by a private note to Colonel Thomas asking him to destroy it.

[No. 96.] FORT SUMTER, S. C., *April* 8, 1861.
Col. L. THOMAS,
    Adjutant-General, U. S. Army.

COLONEL: I have the honor to report that the resumption of work yesterday (Sunday) at various points on Morris Island, and the vigorous prosecution of it this morning, apparently strengthening nearly all the batteries which are under the fire of our guns, show that they either have received some news from Washington which has put them on the *qui vive*, or that they have received orders from Montgomery to commence operations here. I am preparing by the side of my barbette guns protection for our men from the shells, which will be almost continuously bursting over or in our work.

I had the honor to receive by yesterday's mail the letter of the honorable Secretary of War, dated April 4, and confess that what he there states surprises me very greatly, following as it does, and contradicting so positively, the assurance Mr. Crawford telegraphed he was authorized to make. I trust that this matter will be at once put in a correct light, as a movement made now, when the South has been erroneously informed that none such will be attempted, would produce most disastrous results throughout our country.

It is, of course, now too late for me to give any advice in reference to the proposed scheme of Captain Fox. I fear that its result cannot fail to be disastrous to all concerned. Even with his boat at our walls, the loss of life (as I think I mentioned to Mr. Fox) in unloading her will more than pay for the good to be accomplished by the expedition, which keeps us, if I can maintain possession of this work, out of position, surrounded by strong works, which must be carried to make this fort of the least value to the United States Government.

We have not oil enough to keep a light in the lantern for one night. The boats will have, therefore, to rely at night entirely upon other marks. I ought to have been informed that this expedition was to come. Colonel Lamon's remark convinced me that the idea, merely hinted at to me by Captain Fox, would not be carried out. We shall strive to do our duty, though I frankly say that my heart is not in the war which I see is to be thus commenced. That God will still avert it, and cause us to resort to pacific measures to maintain our rights, is my ardent prayer.

I am, Colonel, very respectfully,

Your obedient servant,

ROBERT ANDERSON,
Major, First Artillery, Commanding.

In a previous letter Major Anderson had reproached the War Department for leaving him, after nearly forty years' service, without orders, intelligence, or advice.

It is on the the strength of the expression, " I frankly say that my heart is not in the war," that General Doubleday accuses General Anderson of want of loyalty and of being pro-slavery in sympathy.

It so happens that after nearly forty years of faithful service, the fame of that officer has come to rest on one episode of his life—his defence of Moultrie and Sumter. He fought bravely in the Black Hawk, the Seminole, and the Mexican wars. He served with distinction on the staff of Lieut.-General Scott. He wrote several useful works for his branch of the service, and did as much hard work as any officer of his day ; yet if it can be made to appear that he was weak, unwise, or wicked in the performance of his last great trust, then his long years of honorable toil will have been in vain, for it is always the last important act that gives tone and color to the picture of our lives.

No wonder he used the expression attributed to him. For months he had been isolated. He felt deserted and sacrificed. He had seen the ebb-tide of patriotism, and the shoals and quicksands it left around him ; he did not know of the mighty tidal wave of national feeling that had commenced its flow. What wonder was it that he was sick at heart? Brutus at Philippi shrank for a moment before the premonition of his doom. Peter denied his Master, and the Master himself upon the cross cried out : " Eli, Eli, lama sabachthani? "

Who did not recoil from that prospect that appalled Webster,—" of States dissevered, discordant, belligerent ; of a land rent with civil feuds, and drenched, it may be, in fraternal blood ? "

There was not an honest and patriotic man in the country who did not dread to see the war begun. And of all sorts and conditions of men the soldier best knows the horrors of war, and is most unwilling to see his own country subjected to its miseries. Of course their finer feelings are blunted in the heat of action.

> " The blood more stirs to rouse a lion
> Than to start a hare."

No one has ever claimed that the siege of Sumter was at all remarkable in a military sense. It was a moral and not a military crisis.

The Count of Paris says of General Anderson, that " he showed a great moral courage—a very rare thing in revolutions."

The government hesitated to strike, and let

I dare not wait upon I would. It hesitated and temporized, apparently weighing small physical advantages against the prestige of moral right. It seemed at first more inclined to follow the Macchiavellian policy of Louis XI, rather than the braver example of Themistocles.

But Anderson's action changed all this. The struggle inaugurated at Sumter ended in a great revolution.

In this contest, while the South was in rebellion, it was the North that forced the revolution.

Formerly we had only a Union of States, now we have a United People. Formerly we claimed to be a nation only by the consent of Sovereign members bound by artificial ties; now we claim to be a Sovereign People developed through psychological laws.

Like other nations we are beginning to have an autonomy of action and a political equation.

The next and not less important feature in our Revolution was the abolition of slavery. We cast out that unclean thing, because it had become heterogeneous and hateful. We placed the higher law of Equality in our Constitution, because it was of endogenous growth. This necessity for a change in our government had grown out of a change in our character as a people. Such a time in a nation's life is like a crisis in a disease. A nation that cannot stand it, disintegrates. We have had our trial and tragedy, and bitter and bloody it was. But now that the issue is settled, we should criticise the events of the time and the men of that hour with all possible fairness.

There is glory enough for all. And although those who came at the eleventh hour should receive their reward, even as those who came at the first, yet the nation will not forget those who were the first to stand firm, and who were faithful among the faithless and faithful to the end.

CHAPTER II.

IF the familiar statement were renewed that Republican governments have produced more than their share of the great men of history, it would be accepted as a truism by nearly all readers of the English-speaking race. If a second thought were given to the proposition, the heroes of Plutarch, and the Hampdens and Cromwells, the Washingtons and Lincolns of modern times would be passed in almost unconscious mental review as a satisfactory illustration of the assumption. Yet all thoughtful men of our time know that there is a reverse to our Democratic medallion.

If very heroic qualities are developed in our times of trial, very undesirable qualities are manifested in our seasons of prosperity. That majorities can be as despotic as crowned kings, is pretty generally conceded. That popular opinion is as impatient of contradiction as the most pedantic pedagogue, seems to be as unde-

niably true. Hence it too often happens that
in republics there is a certain duplicity or ti-
midity in criticism, if the question to be examined
is one about which a popular opinion has been
formed.

Mr. John Stuart Mill was asked on the hust-
ings, on the only occasion on which he stood
for Parliament, if he had not said that the British workingmen were given to lying. Mr. Mill
said, unhesitatingly, that he had. The British
mob were generous enough to cheer him. No
doubt they consoled themselves with the thought
that, on Falstaff's authority, the whole world
was given to the same practice.

The American public have not been accused
of this fault, yet, in discussing the causes and
purposes of our late civil war, there is a very
politic, yet positive, *suppressio veri.*

We all talk and write as if our fore-thoughts
had been the same as our after-thoughts. In
the hurley-burley of the present we forget the
passions and prejudices of the past. There
seems to be a quiet assumption on the part
of most middle-aged men that their political
opinions have not changed since the rebel guns
opened on Sumter. We are all political prophets, but, unfortunately, prophets after the facts.

Nearly all men condemn slavery now. This

is right and proper. The image of Dagon is overthrown. Who ever worshipped Dagon? No man. It is a safe and pleasant thing to revile a blind and helpless Samson.

If our elections are any index to popular opinion, the great majority of voters in this country up to 1860 either did not believe that slavery was wrong or were indifferent to it as a political issue. If Mr. Lincoln had proclaimed on the 4th of March, 1861, that he was about to wage a war for the suppression of slavery, in all human probability his administration would have proved an utter failure.[1]

There is one thing in connection with our civil war that we have almost forgotten, and which future historians are likely to overlook. It is, that the cause of the gravest apprehension to all thoughtful men and women in all parts of our country was at that time the fear of a servile insurrection in the South. Undoubtedly one of the gravest sins the rebel leaders have to answer for is, that in bringing on the war,

---

[1] The Abolition party so late as the Presidental election of 1852 only numbered 156,149 (Hale's vote), out of a total of 3,144,201 votes cast.

It was often mentioned as a matter of ridicule or reproach during the war, that the original abolitionists were rarely found at the front. It cannot be fairly assumed that this fact proves their insincerity. A large proportion of these fanatics were preachers, scholars, quakers, or aged men, whose age, infirmities, or callings prevented them from becoming military crusaders in the cause. I do not doubt that Giddings, Garrison, or Wendell Phillips would have died at the stake rather than denied their abolition sentiments.

they risked this fate for their misguided fol-
lowers.

I can state on the best possible authority that
General Anderson dreaded this possibility with
the most painful intensity. And why was this
apprehension not realized? Simply and solely
because slavery degraded and emasculated the
black race more than we thought.[1]

If, for instance, the slaves had retained the
courage and wild spirit of freedom of the Zulu
Kaffirs, who does not know that there would
have been a holocaust of houses, barns, and
bridges all through the South, as soon as the
Federal soldiers crossed the Potomac? What
murders, torturings, and ravishings would there
not have been had a black Spartacus arisen in
every Southern State! Is this mere theorizing?
Ask the people of Northern Minnesota what
atrocities the Sioux committed when they took
the war-path in 1863. And the provocation of

---

[1] I am indebted for this statement and the deduction made from it,
to Gov. Chas. Anderson, the sole surviving brother of Gen. Robert
Anderson.

About the time of the bombardment of Sumter, Gov. Anderson
made a Union speech in San Antonio, Texas, during the delivery of
which his life was repeatedly threatened by armed desperadoes, who
were enraged by his vehement denunciation of the rebel leaders.

He was subsequently imprisoned by Gen. Ben. McCollough, C. S.
A., but made a remarkable escape into Mexico. He made his way
back to Ohio, and was commissioned Colonel of the 63d Ohio Inft.
He was wounded at Stone River, ran on the Republican ticket for
Lieut. Governor of Ohio, was elected by a 100,000 majority, and suc-
ceeded Brough as governor on his death in 1865.

the worst-used Indian tribe we ever cheated
out of home and lands was mild as moonlight
compared to the curse and wrong of slavery.

Fortunately, these apprehensions were not
realized. But we can not fairly judge of the men
who were prominent actors in the first act of
our Rebellion, without analyzing all the considerations that influenced them at that time.

The abolition of slavery was not one of the
objects, but one of the accidents, of the war.
We may say now that it would have been a
justifiable and praiseworthy object ; yet this is
an after-thought.

It must be stated, in all fairness, that although
a great many people thought slavery was wrong,
even before our war, yet so strong was the rev-
erence for the written law, that but few would
have risked a war to abolish it.

The object of the war is generally and more
properly stated to have been the preservation
of the Union.   Admitting that this was its object, it must now be admitted that there was an
accidental consequence more important even
than the perpetuation of the Union.

As before stated, it is our union as a people.

The war established the paramount claim of
the general government on the personal al-
legiance of every man in the country.

It established the right of the government to
punish every man in the country for a violation
of its laws.   Mr. Calhoun claimed that a State
could throw the ægis of its protection over any
citizen, and thus nullify the power of the general government.   This will never be seriously
claimed again.

It has established for us as a *fact* that which
was once held by a few as a metaphysical theory, that the true principle of nationality is the
cohesive power of race.

This may seem to be a merely plausible plati-
tude.   Yet it is a self-evident deduction.   People of the same race, when living contiguously,
will, of course, speak the same language.   Under this great bond of union, they are likely to
be subject to the influence of the same laws and
literature.   Consequently, their tastes and am-
bitions will be given the same bent.   Living
and laboring under the same conditions, they
will have the same temptations to vice, the same
incentives to virtue.   They will find it to their
advantage to combine in business enterprises,
and this can only be successfully done by people
who speak the same language and have been
raised in the same way.   In fine, masses of
men moving in the same direction and under
similar conditions have to combine.

There were many of the last generation who thought they could escape the effect of this law of race. We know now that any community which would claim independent action in the midst of any of the great nationalities of our day would suffer annihilation. The time when dynasties and factions can stand in the way of national progress, or interfere with the autonomous action of a race, is past.

Without considering these facts and weighing these considerations, we cannot fairly estimate the political problem of Sumter.

It was not a question of blood and bones, and bricks and mortar.

> " It *was not* all of life to live,
> Nor all of death to die."

A question of national existence, and, more than that, of national character, hung upon the issue.

From the time Major Anderson went to Fort Moultrie to the time he left Sumter, it is hard to characterize the course of both the Buchanan and the Lincoln administrations in dignified yet appropriate terms. Now that their despatches have been published, it is evident that both administrations wished that officer to relieve them of responsibility by taking his own course.

Probably neither could have relieved Sumter without risking the safety of Washington. Nor could they abandon without sacrificing a principle, so both temporized and left the garrison of Sumter to its fate. [1]

If Major Anderson had disobeyed his orders and fought, he would have been whipped. Then he could have been made a scape-goat, and cashiered. Had he capitulated before a fight, he would have been equally open to censure.

He felt that he was badly treated and said so, yet in spite of this, and in disregard of personal sympathies and friendships, he was true to his duty.

When Marshal Bazaine was tried for treason, he said, in the course of his trial, that after the Emperor Napoleon was dethroned he did not know what to do. " What! " asked the Duc D'Aumale, the president of his court-martial, " did France then cease to exist? "

Major Anderson had no such doubts. He knew he had a country to cherish, love, and defend, in spite of mistakes and vacillations of Cabinets and leaders. After the first overt act of war, after he had to deal with facts, the great mind of Abraham Lincoln asserted itself. From

[1] See Addenda.

that time on we had nothing to be ashamed of. From that time on we had grand, not petty, war; statesmanship, not statecraft.

As stated in the beginning, the political conspiracies which preceded our civil war of 1861 were the consequences and not the causes of the conflicting interests which made the contest inevitable. However spontaneous the outburst of revolutions and rebellions may appear, their force must at first be directed by conspirators. For, to overthrow an established government, force is required, combination is essential, and secrecy is a necessity. Otherwise all such attempts would be suppressed in their inception.

It was on the 5th of January, 1861, the day that the *Star of the West* started for the relief of Sumter, that the Southern leaders in Washington held their secret caucus in which they organized their rebellion. This course had been determined long before, but it was on this occasion that these four resolutions were adopted. To wit:

1st. The cotton States should secede immediately.

2d. Delegates should be chosen to meet in Montgomery, Ala., on Feb. 15th, to organize a provisional government.

3d. That the conspirators should remain in the Federal Congress during the Buchanan Administration, to obstruct coercive legislation ; and

4th. Davis, Mallory, and Slidell were appointed a committee to carry out the objects of the meeting.

That their conspiracies utterly failed was owing to the fact, which was so impressively stated by Mr. Webster in the Senate in 1850, " that the machinations of men are powerless against the laws of nature."

Under the directive force of moral laws the balance between the centrifugal and centripetal forces of our political system seems to be reestablished, and let us hope that in the future, as in the past, " Treason can but peep to what it would."

THE END.

ADDENDA.

Reports of Generals Anderson and Beauregard of the bombardment and evacuation of Fort Sumter.

TELEGRAM.

STEAMSHIP *Baltic*, OFF SANDY HOOK,
April 18 (1861), 10:30 A.M. *via* NEW YORK.

Having defended Fort Sumter for thirty-four hours, until the quarters were entirely burned, the main gates destroyed by fire, the gorge walls seriously injured, the magazine surrounded by flames, and its door closed from the effect of heat, four barrels and three cartridges of powder only being available, and no provisions remaining but pork, I accepted terms of evacuation offered by General Beauregard, being the same offered by him on the 11th inst., prior to the commencement of hostilities, and marched out of the fort Sunday afternoon, the 14th inst., with colors flying and drums beating, bringing away company and private property, and saluting my flag with fifty guns.

ROBERT ANDERSON,
Major First Artillery, *Commanding.*

Hon. S. CAMERON,
Secretary of War, Washington.

REPLY.

WAR DEPARTMENT, WASHINGTON,
April 20, 1861.

Major ROBERT ANDERSON,
   Late Commanding at Fort Sumter :

MY DEAR SIR.—I am directed by the President of the
United States to communicate to you, and through you
to the officers and men of your command at Forts Moultrie and Sumter, the approbation of the government of
your and their judicious and gallant conduct there, and
to tender you and them the thanks of the government
for the same.

SIMON CAMERON,
Secretary of War.

GENERAL BEAUREGARD'S REPORT.

HDQRS. PROVISIONAL ARMY, CHARLESTON, S. C.
April 27, 1861.

SIR.—I have the honor to submit the following detailed
report of the bombardment and surrender of Fort Sumter and the incidents connected therewith.   Having completed my channel defences and batteries in the harbor
necessary for the reduction of Fort Sumter, I dispatched
two of my aids at 2:20 P.M., on Thursday, the 11th of
April, with a communication to Major Anderson, in command of the fortification, demanding its evacuation.   I
offered to transport himself and command to any port in
the United States he might elect, to allow him to move
out of the fort with company arms and property and all
private property, and to salute his flag in lowering it.   He
refused to accede to the demand.   As my aids were
about leaving, Major Anderson remarked that if we did

not batter him to pieces he would be starved out in a few days, or words to that effect. This being reported to me by my aids on their return with his refusal at 5:10 P.M., I deemed it proper to telegraph the purport of his remark to the Secretary of War. In reply I received by telegraph the following instructions at 9:10 P.M.

" Do not desire needlessly to bombard Fort Sumter. If Major Anderson will state the time at which, as indicated by him, he will evacuate, and agree that in the meantime he will not use his guns against us unless ours should be employed against Fort Sumter, you are authorized thus to avoid effusion of blood. If this, or its equivalent, be refused, reduce the fort as your judgment decides most practicable."

At 1 P.M. I sent my aids with a communication to Major Anderson, based on the foregoing instructions. It was placed in his hands at 12:45 A.M., 12th inst. He expressed his willingness to evacuate the fort on Monday at noon, if provided with the necessary means of transportation, and if he should not receive contradictory instructions from his government or additional supplies, but he declined to agree not to open his guns on us in the event of any hostile demonstrations on our part against his flag. This reply, which was opened and shown to my aids, plainly indicated that if instructions should be received contrary to his purpose to evacuate, or if he should receive his supplies, or if the Confederate troops should fire on hostile troops of the United States, or upon transports bearing the United States flag, containing men, munitions, and supplies designed for hostile operations against us, he would still feel himself bound to fire upon us, and to hold possession of the fort. As in consequence of a communication from the President of the United States to the governor of South Carolina, we were in momentary expectation of an attempt to reinforce Fort Sumter, or of a descent upon our coast to that end from the United States fleet then lying at the entrance of the harbor, it was manifest by an imperative necessity to reduce the port as speedily as possible, and not to wait until the ships and the fort should unite in a combined attack upon us. Accordingly my aids, carrying out my instructions, promptly refused to accede to the terms proposed by Major Anderson, and notified him in writing that our batteries would open on Fort Sumter in one hour. This notification was given at 3:20 A.M. of Friday the 12th instant. The signal shell was fired at Fort Johnson at 4:30 A.M. At about 5 o'clock the fire of our batteries became general. Fort Sumter did not open fire until 7 o'clock, when it commenced with a vigorous fire upon the Cummings' Point iron battery. The enemy next directed his fire upon the enfilade battery on Sullivan's Island, constructed to sweep the parapet of Fort Sumter, to prevent the working of the barbette guns, and to dismount them. This was also the aim of the floating battery, the Dalhgren battery, and the gun batteries at Cummings' Point. The enemy next opened on Fort Moultrie, between which and Fort Sumter a steady and almost constant fire was kept up throughout the day. These three points—Fort Moultrie, Cummings' Point, and the end of Sullivan's Island, where the floating battery, Dahlgren battery, and the enfilade battery were placed—were the points to which the enemy seemed almost to confine his attention, although he fired a number of shots at Captain Butler's mortar battery, situated to the east of Fort Moultrie, and a few at Captain James' mortar batteries at Fort Johnson. During the day (12th instant) the fire of my batteries was kept up most spiritedly, the guns and mortars being worked in the coolest manner, preserving

the prescribed intervals of firing. Toward evening it became evident that our fire was very effective, as the enemy
was driven from his barbette gun which he attempted to
work in the morning, and his fire was confined to his
casemated guns, but in a less active manner than in the
morning, and it was observed that several of his guns *en
barbette* were disabled. During the whole of Friday night
our mortar batteries continued to throw shells, but, in
obedience to orders, at longer intervals. The night was
rainy and dark ; and as it was almost confidently expected
that the United States fleet would attempt to land troops
upon the islands or to throw men into Fort Sumter by
means of boats, the greatest vigilance was observed at all
our channel batteries, and by our troops on both Morris
and Sullivan's islands.

Early on Saturday morning all our batteries reopened
upon Fort Sumter, which responded vigorously for a time,
directing its fire specially against Fort Moultrie. About
8 o'clock A.M., smoke was seen issuing from the quarters
of Fort Sumter. Upon this the fire of our batteries was
increased, as a matter of course, for the purpose of
bringing the enemy to terms as speedily as possible, inas-
much as his flag was still floating defiantly above him.
Fort Sumter continued to fire from time to time, but at
long and irregular intervals, amid the dense smoke, flying
shot, and bursting shell. Our brave troops, carried away
by their natural, generous impulses, mounted the different batteries, and at every discharge from the fort cheered
the garrison for its pluck and gallantry, and hooted the
fleet lying inactive just outside the bar.

About 1.30 P.M., it being reported to me that the flag
was down (it afterward appeared that the flag-staff had
been shot away), and the conflagration, from the large
volume of smoke being apparently on the increase, I sent
three of my aids with a message to Major Anderson to

the effect that, seeing his flag no longer flying, his quarters in flames, and supposing him to be in distress, I desired to offer him any assistance he might stand in need of. Before my aids reached the fort the United States flag was displayed on the parapet, but remained there only a short time when it was hauled down and a white flag substituted in its place. When the United States flag first disappeared, the firing from our batteries almost entirely ceased, but reopened with increased vigor when it reappeared on the parapet, and was continued until the white flag was raised, when it entirely ceased. Upon the arrival of my aids at Fort Sumter they delivered their message to Major Anderson, who replied that he thanked me for my offer, but desired no assistance. Just previous to their arrival Col. Wigfall, one of my aids, who had been detached for special duty on Morris Island, had, by order of Brigadier-Gen. Simons, crossed over to Fort Sumter from Cummings' Point, in an open boat, with private Gourdin Young, amidst a heavy fire of shot and shell, for the purpose of ascertaining from Major Anderson whether his intention was to surrender, his flag being down and his quarters in flames. On reaching the fort the colonel had an interview with Major Anderson, the result of which was that Major Anderson understood him as offering the same conditions on the part of General Beauregard as had been tendered him on the 11th instant, while Colonel Wigfall's impression was that Major Anderson unconditionally surrendered, trusting to the generosity of General Beauregard to offer such terms as would be honorable and acceptable to both parties. Meanwhile, before these circumstances were reported to me, and in fact as soon as the aids I had dispatched with offers of assistance had set out on their mission, hearing that a white flag was flying over the fort, I sent Major Jones, my chief-of-staff, and some other aids, with substantially the same propositions I had submitted to Major Anderson on the 11th inst., with the exception of the privilege of saluting his flag. The Major (Anderson) replied : "it would be exceedingly gratifying to him, as well as his command, to be permitted to salute their flag, having so gallantly defended the fort under such trying circumstances, and hoped that General Beauregard would not refuse it, as such privilege was not unusual." He further said he "would not urge the point, but would prefer to refer the matter to me." The point was, therefore, left open until the matter was submitted to me. Previous to the return of Major Jones, I sent a fire-engine, under Mr. M. H. Nathan, chief of the fire department, and Surgeon-General Gibbes of South Carolina, with several of my aids, to offer further assistance to the garrison of Fort Sumter, which was declined. I very cheerfully agreed to allow the salute, as an honorable testimony to the gallantry and fortitude with which Major Anderson and his command had defended their fort, and I informed Major Anderson of my decision about $7\frac{1}{2}$ o'clock, through Major Jones, my chief-of-staff.

The arrangements being completed, Major Anderson embarked with his command on the transport prepared to convey him to the United States fleet lying outside the bar, and the troops immediately garrisoned the fort, and before sunset the flag of the Confederate States floated over the ramparts of Fort Sumter.

> *   *   *   *   *   * [1]

I am, sir, very respectfully,
Your obedient servant,
G. T. BEAUREGARD,
Brigadier-General Com'dg.

Hon. L. P. WALKER,
Secretary of War.

---

[1] The omitted part embraced only compliments to his command.

APPENDIX.

The Confederate leaders profited by the lesson given by Major Anderson in his seizure of Sumter, by taking the forts within their borders, either before they passed their ordinance of secession or a few days after. In most instances Messrs. Floyd and Cooper had taken care that good reliable rebels were in command at important posts.

A brief résumé may be interesting as a reminiscence.

Georgia passed its ordinance of secession January 19, 1861.

Fort Pulaski was seized on January 3d ; Augusta Arsenal, January 24th ; Oglethorp Barracks and Fort Jackson, on January 26th.

Fort Pulaski was in charge of Captain Wm. II. C. Whiting, Capt. of U. S. Engineers, born in the State of Maine ; subsequently General Whiting, C. S. A., Chief Engineer in Charleston Harbor, and later on at Fort Fisher.

Augusta Arsenal was garrisoned by Captain Elzey, 2d Artillery, and his company. Captain Elzey surrendered without firing a shot, and became General Elzey, C. S. A.

It was also the painful duty of Captain Whiting to report the surrender of Oglethorp Barracks and of Fort Jackson.

An ordinance of secession was adopted in Mississippi on January 9th, and in Alabama on January 11, 1861.

The arsenal at Mount Vernon was seized by State troops January 4th, and Forts Morgan and Gaines on the 5th.

Governor Moore, of Alabama, wrote to his Excellency James Buchanan as follows : "Sir : In a spirit of frankness I hasten to inform you by letter that, by my order, the above-named forts and arsenal have been *peacefully* occupied and are now held by the troops of the State of Alabama.

* * * * * * * *

"I deem it my duty to take every precautionary step to make the secession of the State peaceful, and prevent detriment to my people.

* * * * * * * *

"The purpose with which my order was given, and has been executed, was to avoid and not to provoke hostilities between the State and Federal governments." (Page 327, "Confederate Correspondence.") And so on for quantity.

Imagine the Fenians seizing Dublin Castle with these excuses.

Florida voted on the ordinance of secession on January 10th. The result could not have been known for a week, yet the arsenal at Apalachicola was seized on January 6th; Fort Marion, St. Augustine, January 7th; Barrancas Barracks, Forts Barrancas and McKee, and the Pensacola Navy Yard were seized, and the surrender of Fort Pickens was demanded, on the 12th.

In the Confederate correspondence in relation to Florida, p. 348, *et seq.*, there is some interesting reading.

First we find a request of Senator Yulee to the Secretary of War, asking a list of army officers from Florida, with rank and pay. The information was given by Secretary Floyd. Next we find a request of Yulee and Mallory for the number of U. S. troops in Florida, and the amount of arms and ammunition in all the forts and arsenals of the State. A paper giving the desired information in full was made out by the Ordnance Department. But on January 9th it suddenly occurred to Secretary of War Holt, that "the interests of the service forbid that the information which you ask should at this moment be made public."

One fort and one arsenal had already been forcibly seized, a few days before, by the constituents of the Honorable Senators.

The U. S. steamer *Brooklyn* arrived off Pensacola with reinforcements for Fort Pickens on February 6, 1861.

These troops were kept on board the steamer by a secret understanding with the rebels, called an informal truce, from that date to the 12th of April, when they were landed.

On the 23d of January, 1861, a special messenger of the government, Lieutenant Saunders, was arrested as a prisoner of war at Pensacola.

January 26th, Secretary Holt telegraphs General Scott: "The President is much disturbed by a telegraphic despatch which announces that the *Brooklyn* has sailed with two companies instead of one as ordered." (Vol. 1, p. 454, "Rebellion Record.")

On the same page we have the explanation of the disturbance of the Executive intellect.

"PENSACOLA, *January* 28, 1861.

"To Hon. JOHN SLIDELL, or, in his absence, Hon. R. W. HUNTER, or Governor BIGLER :

"We hear the *Brooklyn* is coming with reinforcements for Fort Pickens. No attack on its garrison is contemplated, but, on the contrary, we desire to keep the peace, and if the present status be preserved we will guarantee that no attack will be made upon it, but if reinforcements be attempted, resistance and a bloody conflict seem inevitable. Should the government thus attempt to augment its force —when no possible call for it exists, when we are preserving a peaceful policy—an assault may be made upon the fort at a moment's warning. All preparations are made. Our whole force—1,700 strong—will regard it as a hostile act. Impress this upon the President, and urge that the inevitable consequence of reinforcement under present circumstances is instant war, as peace will be preserved if no reinforcements be attempted. If the President wants an assurance of all I say from Colonel Chase, commanding the forces, I will transmit it at once. I am determined to stave off war if possible. Answer promptly.

"S. R. Mallory."

It is evident that Slidell, Hunter, & Co. had anticipated Senator Mallory's suggestions.

The despatch, which was sent by Lieut. Saunders to Commodore Armstrong, and which was taken from him by force, was in words and figures as follows:

"Washington, *January* 29, 1861.

"To James Glynn, commanding the *Macedonian;* Capt. W. S. Walker, commanding the *Brooklyn,* and other naval officers in command; and Lieut. Adam J. Slemmer, First Regiment Artillery, U. S. Army, commanding Fort Pickens, Pensacola, Fla.:

"In consequence of the assurances received from Mr. Mallory in a telegram of yesterday to Messrs. Slidell, Hunter, and Bigler, with a request it should be laid before the President, that Fort Pickens would not be assaulted, and an offer of such an assurance to the same effect from Colonel Chase, for the purpose of avoiding a hostile collision, upon receiving satisfactory assurances from Mr. Mallory and Colonel Chase that Fort Pickens will not be attacked, you are instructed not to land the company on board the *Brooklyn* unless said fort shall be attacked or preparations shall be made for its attack. The provisions necessary for the supply of the fort you will land. The *Brooklyn* and other vessels of war on the station will remain, and you will exercise the utmost vigilance and be prepared at a moment's warning to land the company at Fort Pickens, and you and they will instantly repel an attack on the fort.

"The President yesterday sent a special message to Congress commending the Virginia resolution of compromise. The Commissioners of different States are to meet here on Monday, the 4th February, and it is important that during their session a collision of arms should be avoided, unless an attack should be made or there should be preparation for such an attack. In either event the *Brooklyn* and the other vessels will act promptly.

"Your right, and that of the other officers in command at Pensacola, freely to communicate with the government by special messenger, and its right in the same manner to communicate with yourself and them, will remain intact as the basis on which the present instruction is given.

"J. Holt, *Secretary of War.*
"Isaac Toucey, *Secretary of the Navy.*"

This was the basis of the famous truce under which the Confederates erected batteries all around Pickens, as they did about Sumter. It was on the 1st of April that General Scott signed the order placing Bvt. Lieut.-Colonel Harvey Brown in command of the secret expedition for the relief of Fort Pickens, of which the *Powhatan* formed a part.

The following extracts from General Meig's letter to General Totten, p. 394, partly explain the *Powhatan* mystery:

"The uncertainty of the government as to the condition of Fort Pickens, and as to the very orders and instructions under which the squadron off that fortress was acting, led to apprehensions lest the place might be taken before relief could reach it.

"A landing in boats from the mainland on a stormy night was perfectly practicable, in spite of the utmost efforts of a fleet anchored outside and off the bar to prevent it. Such a landing in force, taking possession of the low flank embrasures by men armed with revolvers, would be likely to sweep in a few minutes over the ramparts of Fort Pickens, defended by only forty soldiers and forty ordinary men from the navy yard, a force which did not allow one man to be kept at each flanking gun.

"Believing that a ship-of-war could be got ready for sea and reach Pensacola before any expedition in force, I advised the sending of such a ship under a young and energetic commander, with orders to enter the harbor without stopping, and, once in, to prevent any boat expedition from the main to Santa Rosa.

"Capt. David D. Porter readily undertook this dangerous duty, and, proceeding to New York, succeeded in fitting out the *Powhatan*, and sailed on the 6th for his destination.

* * * * * * *

"On the morning of the 17th, while engaged in landing the horses, the *Powhatan*, which we had passed without seeing her during the voyage, hove in sight. A note from Colonel Brown advised me that in his opinion her entrance into the harbor at that time would bring on a collision, which it was very important to defer until our stores, guns, and ammunition were disposed of.

"As the enemy did not seem inclined yet to molest us; as with 600 troops in the fort and three war steamers anchored close inshore, there was no danger of a successful attempt at a landing by the enemy, it was evident that it was important to prevent a collision, and her entrance would have uselessly exposed a gallant officer and a devoted crew to extreme dangers.

"The circumstances had changed since Captain Porter's orders had been issued by the President. Knowing the imperative nature of these orders, and the character of him who bore them, I feared that it would not be possible to arrest his course; but requesting the commander of the *Wyandotte*, on board of which I fortunately found myself at the time I received Colonel Brown's letter, to get under way and place his vessel across the path of the *Powhatan*, making signal that I wished to speak with him, I succeeded at length, in spite of his changes of course and his disregard of our signals, in stopping this vessel, which steered direct for the perilous channel on which frowned the guns of McKee, Barrancas, and many newly constructed batteries.

" I handed to Captain Porter Colonel Brown's letter, indorsed upon it my hearty concurrence in its advice, which, under his authority from the Executive, had the force of an order from the President himself, and brought the *Powhatan* to anchor near the *Atlantic*, in position to sweep with her guns the landing-place and its communications.

" The *Brooklyn* shortly afterward anchored east of the *Atlantic*, and the *Wyandotte* took up position near her."

But why first assign the *Powhatan*, first assigned to the Sumter expedition, and then transferred without the knowledge of either the Secretaries of War or the Navy?

We extract a few interesting extracts from the " Confederate Correspondence," p. 443, *et seq.* :

" I shall give the enemy a shot next week before retiring (from the U. S. Senate). I say *enemy !* Yes, I am theirs, and they are mine. I am willing to be their masters, but not their brothers.

" Yours, in haste,

" D. L. YULEE."

(Oh, shade of Lindley Murray hover o'er us !)

" WASHINGTON, *January* 7, 1861.

" JOSEPH FINEGAN, Esq. (Tallahassee, Fla.):

" MY DEAR SIR : On the other side (following) is a copy of resolutions adopted at a consultation of the Senators from the seceding States, in which Georgia, Alabama, Louisiana, Arkansas, Texas, Mississippi, and Florida were present.

" The idea of the meeting was that the States should go out at once, and provide for an early organization of a Confederate government, not later than 15th February. This time is allowed to enable Louisiana and Texas to participate. It seemed to be the opinion that if we left here, force, loan, and volunteer bills might be passed, which would put Mr. Lincoln in immediate condition for hostilities ; whereas, by remaining in our places until the 4th March, it is thought we can keep the hands of Mr. Buchanan tied, and disable the Republicans from effecting any legislation which will strengthen the hands of the incoming Administration.

*   *   *   *   *   *   *   *

" In haste, yours truly,

" D. L. YULEE."

How secret the Pensacola expedition was may be seen from the following despatches :

"AUGUSTA, *March* 20, 1861.

" President DAVIS :

" My always reliable Washington correspondent says : ' Evident Lincoln intends to reinforce Pickens.'

"WM. H. PRITCHARD."

" WAR DEPARTMENT, A. AND I. G. O.

" MONTGOMERY, *April* 6, 1861.

" Brig.-Gen. BRAXTON BRAGG :

" The government at Washington have determined to reinforce Fort Pickens, and troops are now leaving for that purpose.

" S. COOPER,
"Adjutant and Inspector-General."

North Carolina seceded May 20th. Forts Caswell and Johnston were seized April 16th. The arsenal at Fayetteville was surrendered by Capt. S. S. Anderson, U. S. A., subsequently C. S. A., April 22d. He had forty-two men, but made no resistance.

Louisiana seceded on January 26th. The U. S. arsenal and barracks at Baton Rouge were seized, January 10th ; Forts Jackson and Saint Philip, January 11th; Fort Pike, January 14 ; Fort Macon, January 28th. Paymaster's funds and all government property were soon after taken in New Orleans.

The form of the demand was the same in all cases. To wit : " In the name of the Sovereign State of Louisiana, I now demand," etc., etc.

The ordinance of secession was adopted by the Arkansas Convention, May 6th ; all the U. S. forts and property within the borders of that State and the Indian Territory were seized before the secession of Arkansas.

In Texas no hostile demonstrations were made against the U. S. Government until after the passage of the ordinance of secession, February 1, 1861.

There is only one thing important to note in connection with our subject, and that is, that although General Twiggs, commanding that Department, commenced writing for instructions as early as December 13, 1860, and wrote urgently over and over again, he only received one non-committal letter from General Scott's Aid.

It was evident from the time of his first letter that he did not intend to support the government in coercive measures. In subsequent letters he said that he intended only to be a looker-on, and that he never would fire on an American citizen.

Before the passage of the ordinance of secession Twiggs would probably have collected the troops under his command and marched them to any place the government might have designated.

If, on the other hand, the government wished to hold Texas by force, the troops should of course have been placed under the command of some able and loyal officer, and concentrated at the State capital.

As it was, Twiggs was relieved by Col. Waite, February 19, 1861.

The first letter of instructions to Col. Waite is a military curiosity:

'HEAD-QUARTERS OF THE ARMY,

" WASHINGTON, *February* 4, 1861.

" Col. C. A. WAITE, *U. S. Army,*
" *Commanding Department of Texas, San Antonio :*

" SIR.—The General-in-Chief directs me to write you as follows :
To relieve Brevet Major-General Twiggs, you were put in orders the
28th ultimo to command, according to your brevet rank, the Department of Texas. Instructions followed three days later for sending
the five companies of artillery on the Rio Grande to Brazos Santiago,
there to be embarked in a steamer (ordered hence to meet them),
with their batteries complete, leaving their horses, for sale or other
service, behind. If necessary, the artillery companies will be re-
placed by detachments of infantry, unless Texas should in the meantime have declared herself out of the Union.

" In the latter case you will wait for instructions respecting the disposition of the troops (other than the artillery) under your command
and the public property in their hands, which you will hold and preserve.

" I am, etc.,
" L. THOMAS."

This letter was written not by the traitor Floyd but by the patriot
Holt ; not under the administration of poor Pierce, but under that
of the veteran statesman, James Buchanan.

A department commander is told that instructions will only be
sent him as to his arm of strength *after* the State in which he is commanding may have seceded.

This letter was sent at a time when the government had learned to
its sorrow that secession meant open defiance, spoliation, or war.

" Angels and ministers of grace defend us!"